THE
HOMEMADE
PANTRY

THE
HOMEMADE
PANTRY

101 FOODS YOU CAN
STOP BUYING & START MAKING

ALANA CHERNILA

PHOTOGRAPHS BY JENNIFER MAY

Clarkson Potter/Publishers
New York

For Joey,
Sadie,
and Rosie

"We cannot go back in time. Instead, we must
reinvent life for ourselves."
—LAURIE COLWIN

Copyright © 2012 by Alana Chernila
Photographs copyright © 2012 by Jennifer May

All rights reserved.
Published in the United States by Clarkson Potter/Publishers,
an imprint of the Crown Publishing Group, a division of
Random House, Inc., New York.
www.crownpublishing.com
www.clarksonpotter.com

CLARKSON POTTER is a trademark and POTTER with colophon is
a registered trademark of Random House, Inc.

Library of Congress Cataloging-in-Publication Data
Chernila, Alana.
    The homemade pantry / Alana Chernila.
        p.   cm.
    Includes index.
1. Quick and easy cooking.   2. Convenience foods.   I. Title.
TX833.5.C44   2012
641.5—dc23   2011023000

ISBN 978-0-307-88726-9
eISBN 978-0-307-95326-1

Printed in China

Design by Stephanie Huntwork
Cover design by Stephanie Huntwork
Cover photography by Jennifer May
Food styling by Jessica Bard
Prop styling by Kari Chapin

First Edition

CONTENTS

introduction

THIS IS MY KITCHEN. Come on in, but be prepared—it might not be quite what you expect.

There is flour on the counter, oats that overflowed onto the floor, chocolate-encrusted spoons in the sink. There is Joey, the husband, exhausted by the preschoolers who were hanging on him all day, and he is stuffing granola into his mouth to ease his five o'clock starvation. There are two little girls trying to show me cartwheels in that minuscule space between the refrigerator and the counter where I really need to be. Sadie's seven, and she is asking about the menu and ordering her sister to take over her job of setting the table. Rosie is five, and has already decided that she doesn't want what's for dinner. All I can do is throw up my hands in the midst of it all, and I can almost feel the anxiety of all families trying to get food on the table. Whatever time it is, it is the unfortunate hour that comes over many households right before dinner and links so many of us.

On this night, we're having lasagne, and there are large floppy noodles hanging on the laundry drying rack in the corner. For the filling, there is ricotta in the fridge from a morning cheese-making demonstration that I gave, and I still have milk left for the best part—quick mozzarella. Rosie changes into her tutu every day as soon as she drops her schoolbag, and I zip up her costume with one hand as I massage the hot cheese curds into stretchy mozzarella with the other. I can't help but curse as I realize that I have submerged my hand into nearly boiling whey. "Mommy said 'shit'!" Sadie announces with

a triumphant little dance, and I say it again when I realize that the sauce that I have thrown together from my tomatoes that I roasted and then froze has boiled over.

I could have avoided this whole chaotic event. Any number of companies would have been happy to offer me a frozen lasagne, perfectly boxed into an aluminum pan with easy-to-read instructions. For extra nutrition and crunch, I could have picked up a salad in a bag and a bottle of dressing, and we would have been set. The kitchen would have been clean, dinner would have been ready at a decent hour without the rush, I would have finally had a chance to answer some e-mails, and this day would have been a bit simpler.

So why is there no perfectly boxed lasagne in my oven? At this moment, I must admit that I am asking myself the very same question.

Fortunately, the answer eventually comes to me. When the lasagne mess reaches its pinnacle, something shifts. The smell of the bubbling sauce takes over the kitchen, and Rosie realizes that mozzarella is in the works. She stops mid-cartwheel, puts an apron over her tutu, pulls her stool to the counter, and stands ready to roll the hot cheese into little balls. She'll eat her weight in homemade cheese before the lasagne even goes into the oven. Sadie sets napkins and forks on the table as Joey emerges from his hunger stupor; he is finally aware of the goings-on in the kitchen. "Lasagne?" he asks with hope. With a nod of my head, his whole mood changes, and he spoons my sauce into the glass baking pan so that it can be ready for the first layer of noodles.

In 2003, Joey and I threw ourselves a wedding in the dead of winter. We were both twenty-three, just a few months away from the birth of our first child, and we had three hundred dollars to feed sixty-five hungry and excited people who had traveled the country through snow and ice to witness our nuptials. In a late burst of inspiration, we asked several friends to make what they thought was the perfect lasagne. So on that snowy day, although we didn't even have tables to eat it on, we had the most lovely assortment of pasta and cheese and sauce that I could have dreamed of. With that meal in our laps on folding chairs in my grandfather's house, lasagne became the food of love, support, and warmth for our family.

I thought lasagne couldn't get any better than that, and in many ways, it never can. But then I learned how to make fresh noodles and I made sauce from my own oddly shaped tomatoes and herbs, and I thought it couldn't get any better than that. And then I learned how to turn milk into the silkiest ricotta with a squeeze of lemon and a bit of patience at the stove. Then there was the homemade mozzarella.

AS THE LIST OF THE STAPLES that I make at home has grown, my excitement has moved me to draw friends into my kitchen to create them with me. Of course, we talk about food as we make it, and so often the conversation moves from enthusiasm into another realm, a place filled with guilt and the idea of what we "should" be making in our kitchens. Then there is some version of the same sentiment, punctuated by a heavy sigh.

"I wish I were the kind of person who makes butter."

Tell me, who really is the kind of person who makes butter?

One hundred years ago, many people made their butter every week, patiently churning the yellow gold distilled from the cream of their cow in the backyard. I am a mother of two young children, piecing together work and family the best I can. I have very little time to patiently churn anything. I do, however, make some pretty good butter.

After the birth of our second daughter, driven by a lack of grocery money and some fervent curiosity, I went about trying to learn how to make food from scratch. Joey bought me a yogurt maker for Christmas, and I was so eager to see those cultures in action that I was already heating the milk as the kids opened the rest of their gifts. And like that, I became someone who makes yogurt.

IF WE ARE TO BECOME PEOPLE who do make butter, we might have to shift the way we see ourselves a bit. We might have to get into the adventurous spirit and unearth our own curiosity about where our food comes from. We might have to make a colossal mess of the kitchen. And we might have to slow down, at least long enough to knead a loaf of bread before the day begins. Here are a few reasons I have found myself to be the kind of person who makes butter:

1. Food made at home is better for you.

You know exactly what is going into it, and it will be fresher. There are no preservatives, no chemicals leaching from packaging, and no hidden ingredients.

2. Food made at home tastes better.

Yes, I know that we all have our favorite packaged foods and guilty pleasures, and while you might not be able to re-create all of them, you can make a delicious homemade chocolate sandwich cookie. It will have a deeper chocolate flavor than the one in the blue bag, and it might lack that strange chemical aftertaste you found so addictive as a child. That's probably because that other one has ingredients in it that you wouldn't bring into your home unless you were trying to clean your shower. But I think you'll get addicted to the homemade ones, too—I know I have. Home-blended hot sauce shames the stuff from the store, fresh-baked crackers have a crunch and complexity that far surpasses the alternative, and that's just the beginning.

3. Food made at home usually costs less.

Often, when you buy prepared foods, you are paying for packaging and brand names, shipping, oil, advertising, and who knows what else. If you make the food yourself, you pay only for the raw ingredients.

4. Food made at home eliminates unnecessary packaging.

Have you ever looked at the contents of your garbage or recycling bin? I think you would be shocked at how many wrappers and boxes you get rid of each week.

5. Food made at home will change the way you think about food.

You won't make all of these recipes every week. You might make pickles just once, and then decide that the experience is not for you. But I promise you this—after making *your* pickles, you will think very differently about *all* pickles. After submerging cucumbers in brine you have crafted, you will have closed the distance between yourself and the source of your food. And the closing of this distance can impact your life in ways that I can only begin to predict.

useful tools for the homemade pantry

MONEY, TASTE, AND TIME: IS IT REALLY WORTH IT?

Let's get this out of the way right now. I do not make all of these recipes every week—not even close. I do my best to keep my family eating the best foods possible. Some weeks are filled with all sorts of experimental and lovely treats. My girls might come home to handmade marshmallows in hot chocolate one day and then we might press tortillas together the next day. But some weeks are different, and I'm sure you know the kinds of weeks I'm talking about. Then I have to prioritize, and only the easiest and most important recipes warrant my time: yogurt, granola, and snack bars for the ride home from school. For me, the contemplation of each recipe begins with one simple question.

Is this worth it?

The criteria for answering that question shift depending on who will be serving the food, who will be eating it, and what day it is. Whether you are led by cost, taste, time, or just the thrill of the recipe, do what works for you.

COST · When money is scarce, if I can make the food at home less expensively, then it is absolutely worth it. This is especially true when it comes to foods that my family eats every day, basic staples that I need no matter how tight the grocery budget.

TASTE · Of course, as I bite into my first homemade potato chip or fruit rollup, I can't help but compare its taste to the store-bought equivalent. Does it taste better? Almost always, *yes*. Some won't just be better, they will be so phenomenal that it will be hard to go back to the packaged versions.

TIME · When life is really busy and I can barely find the couple minutes to make a sandwich, the efficiency factor takes over and only the fast and easy recipes are realistic. Even if a recipe far exceeds its store-bought equivalent in cost and taste, it will take a lot for me to commit to a three-hour hands-on prep time. If my kitchen is clean and ready and you want to take my kids for the afternoon, then we'll talk about it.

THRILL · Although this might be the hardest one to put your finger on, it's really the thing that keeps me going. Whether it's your inner pioneer expressing deep satisfaction when you look at your rows of bright-red jam–filled mason jars or your inner five-year-old (or real five-year-old) celebrating when the butter breaks from the buttermilk, the thrill is what keeps me cooking and sharing.

about my recipes

Sometimes there will be a moment in a recipe when the texture of the batter or syrup or dough might seem different from how it should be, or maybe something went wrong and you can't quite figure out where that happened or if you can fix it. I've tried to identify those moments in these recipes—I call them the **tense moments**. You might experience them or you might not, but if you do, I'm hoping my stories and notes will ease a bit of the tension. I often get phone calls from friends who are having tense moments in their own cooking, and together we try to figure out what happened, how to fix it, or if there really is anything wrong. Think of the "tense moments" in these recipes as our phone call when you need them.

MANY RECIPES IN THIS BOOK involve the use of ingredients that you can also make from this book, for example, Buttermilk Ranch Dressing (page 114) requires Buttermilk (page 41), Mayonnaise (page 117), and Yogurt (page 30). In such recipes, I specify homemade *or* store-bought in the ingredient list. I am serious about this—don't feel that your dressing is any less homemade if you use store-bought buttermilk, mayonnaise, and yogurt. **Make what you like, and use what you have.**

IN MY KITCHEN

I am a gadget lover and I have no shame about it. I am not a minimalist in the kitchen. I do not make toast in my oven to avoid the need for a toaster, and the whir of the stand mixer is music to me.

I know that counter space is precious, but if there is a machine or two that you use often, keep it on the counter and it will become infinitely more useful. So many times I'll talk to a friend about my deep love for my food processor, and she'll reply, "I have one of those, but I just don't use it." Inevitably that food processor is tucked behind all sorts of useless items, and as soon as I make the suggestion to let it see the light of day, it goes into regular use.

Certain gadgets will be more necessary for you than others, depending on the recipes that you make regularly and the skills that you feel a machine does better. Most of the recipes in this book can be made without a gadget if that is your preference. When I can, I will describe methods with gadgets and without, but just so you know what's in my kitchen, here is an overview of the tools that I use and suggest in this book.

electric gadgets

AIR POPPER · As surprising as it may be, I think this is the gadget that I have turned people on to the most. Air poppers are easy to find, usually under twenty bucks, and have not improved at all since the 1970s. I love this machine with such ferocity because it makes great popcorn (without oil!) in three minutes. Whenever there is whining and nothing to eat in the house, the popcorn popper comes off the shelf and saves the day.

BLENDER · I use my upright blender for smoothies, milkshakes, and the occasional salad dressing or sauce. I also have an infinitely useful immersion blender—a blender on a stick that I can put right into the pot. I use the immersion blender primarily for blended soups or large batches of tomato sauce or applesauce so that I don't have to transfer batches of soup or sauce from the pot to the blender.

DEHYDRATOR • This is necessary for making fruit rollups and jerkies and some creative snack bars, but it can also be used to dehydrate fruits, berries, herbs, and vegetables. Dehydrators take up a fair amount of space, but they are inexpensive and widen your options for preserving. Some ovens have a dehydrator setting and can go low enough to do the job, and for many foods the sun on a hot rock is a fitting backup.

FOOD PROCESSOR • Cuisinart makes the classic food processor, and I use mine almost every day. The food processor is useful for bread doughs and pie crusts, but where it really shines is as a chopper and grater. The basic blade will chop your nuts and make your salsa, and if you ever have to make carrot cake for 100, the grating disc will take seconds instead of an hour on a box grater. The Cuisinart comes in several sizes, and I have found that the 11-cup is a good size for a family of four.

STAND MIXER • I have a red KitchenAid mixer and I love it like a third child. It's a workhorse that will do whatever I need it to, and I'd say that if you have to have one appliance and you bake, this should be it. There are three basic mixing attachments that come with the mixer: the paddle (looks like a triangle), the wire whip (looks like a whisk), and the dough hook (looks like a hook). I use all three of these attachments,

and I will specify which one to use in each recipe.

YOGURT MAKER • I use a Euro Cuisine yogurt maker. It comes with seven little glass cups that fit perfectly into packed lunches. There are many other yogurt makers out there, and I cannot speak to those I have not used, but I can say that mine has been long lasting and cultures the yogurt in glass, which I find to be pleasing for both health and aesthetic reasons.

non-electric gadgets

FOOD MILL • This is useful for straining skins and seeds out of sauces. The same work can be done by pressing a seedy or skin-filled jam or apple or tomato sauce through a fine-meshed sieve, but the food mill will do it faster, with less effort, and just as quietly. It also does double duty as a baby-food maker, if that is where you are in your life.

MANDOLINE • This will slice your potatoes into perfectly sized chips if you are not so talented with a knife. The slicing blade of a food processor will do similar work, but a mandoline is inexpensive, folds up nicely, and will give you thin and even slices of most fruits and vegetables.

PASTA ROLLER • This fits on the counter with an attached vice to hold the machine steady while you crank the pasta. A pasta roller is such fun to use, and if you have one, you will probably find yourself making fresh pasta more than you ever thought you would. A pasta roller is possible to work with two hands, but much easier with four, so this is a task for which I recruit Joey or the girls.

TORTILLA PRESS • It is impossible for me to get corn tortillas to the thickness that I desire with a rolling pin. A tortilla press solves this problem and saves me tears. If you are lucky enough to live near a Latin grocer, you can usually find a tortilla press for about ten dollars. If you fancy yourself a tortilla maker, I suggest that you make the investment.

other useful tools

CHEESECLOTH • This is essential for most of the cheese recipes in this book and is useful for straining liquids when a sieve is not fine enough. A cheese-making supply store also offers butter muslin, which can be used in place of cheesecloth. Butter muslin is of a finer weave than cheesecloth, and unlike cheesecloth, it is machine washable.

KITCHEN SCALE • Whereas measuring cups are slightly different from kitchen to kitchen, the weight of an ingredient will always be the same. If you weigh your flour, you will know that your 5 ounces will be the same as my 5 ounces. I include weights and cup measures in all of the baking recipes in this book. One cup of all-purpose flour weighs 5 ounces, and this is the standard measurement in my recipes. There are also recipes like Granola (page 48), where a kitchen scale will save you a lot of work and dishwashing. If you set your mixing bowl onto the scale, you can simply

pour the ingredients into the bowl without measuring, taking note of the additional weight on the scale with each ingredient.

THERMOMETER • If you get intimidated by the inclusion of a candy thermometer in a recipe, then it is time that you find the right thermometer (or three!). There are many different kinds of thermometers, and the main differences between them are in the range of temperature that they register and the length of the stem. Here is a quick overview:

candy thermometers have a wide range of temperature (usually between 100°F and 500°F) and have a clip and a longer rod so you can attach them to the side of a pot while the liquid heats. A candy thermometer will often work for cheese-making applications, although sometimes you will be looking for a temperature below 100°F, in which case a cheese thermometer will be more useful.

cheese thermometers range between 40°F and 250°F, and will often be long enough to sit in a stockpot.

meat thermometers have a fairly short rod and they only gauge temperatures between 100°F and 200°F, so they are good for meat and little else.

BEYOND THESE ITEMS, I am assuming that you are starting out with some array of the tools that you prefer. We all find a different meaning for the word *necessary,* but here are some of the other kitchen tools that will be of use for the recipes in this book:

MIXING BOWLS several sizes, at least one very large

LIQUID MEASURING CUPS 2-cup and 4-cup

WOODEN SPOONS

SILICONE SPATULA

ROLLING PIN

FINE-MESHED SIEVES preferably metal, and at least two different sizes

SLOTTED SPOON

KNIVES at least a good chef's knife, a paring knife, and a bread knife

WHISK

JELLY-ROLL PANS (baking sheets with a little lip around the side)

DRY MEASURING CUPS of varied sizes (even if you have a kitchen scale)

MEASURING SPOONS

PARCHMENT PAPER

SIFTER the metal kind (fun for the kids in the kitchen)

SILPAT SILICONE PAN LINER optional but very useful, especially for making some cookies and other sticky items

HOW TO USE YOUR FREEZER

If you are planning to make more basic foods at home, the freezer is your biggest ally.

The freezer section at the grocery store is full of convenient foods, but you can freeze foods yourself with almost as much convenience. After the initial time investment of preparing the food, the only work is remembering to thaw a food before you want to serve or eat it. Most of the foods in this book can be frozen, and I'll give you directions in the storage section of each freezable recipe. Whether you are working with a small freezer attached to your refrigerator or a chest freezer in your basement or garage, you can fill it with fruits, vegetables, and prepared foods.

MEALS • It is almost as easy to make two batches of Lasagne (page 202), Beef Stew (page 138), or Potato Leek Soup (page 136) as it is to make one. Sometimes it makes all of the difference to have a meal ready made. Invest in some good freezer-safe containers, freeze meals in family or individual size portions, and you will always have meal options.

FRUITS AND VEGETABLES • Most vegetables can be blanched and frozen with great success. Blanch, drain, and transfer to freezer bags (see page 168). For fruit, the process is even simpler. Cut the hulls off your strawberries, but other berries are ready as is. Peaches, mangoes, and rhubarb can all be sliced and frozen, and pitted cherries freeze beautifully as well. Lay the whole or sliced fruit in a single layer on a baking sheet and place in the freezer. After two to three hours, the fruit will be frozen and you can store it in freezer bags and lay the bags flat in the freezer.

SNACKS • Use your freezer to extend the shelf life of foods that would normally spoil in the fridge or go stale on the pantry shelf. Cookies, cakes, and most snacks can be frozen in freezer bags or glass freezer containers, and many can be eaten right from the freezer.

WE ALL HAVE different temperaments and talents when it comes to organization, but it pays to keep track of the space in your freezer. Make sure that each container is labeled with the contents and the date you made it, and that you clear out old food regularly. If you have a chest freezer, you can keep a running tally of the contents and their location taped to the top of the freezer so you don't have to spend too long searching for that bag of peas you know is in there.

ricotta
crème fraîche
yogurt
mozzarella
butter
buttermilk
cream cheese

i

IN A WORLD WHERE so much has already been done, it is the first experiences that continue to inspire me. When Rosie was one year old, she sat on my knees, her Alfred Hitchcock cheeks puffed out in their enchanting fashion. She brought her hand to her chest, tilted her head, and said, "Ro!" That her name was her first word made sense to me, as it had mysteriously been her own creation. We had not intended to name her Rosie, but when she emerged into the world with those cheeks (those cheeks!), we had to ditch the name that we had so carefully crafted for her. Joey and I looked at each other, confused, and said in unison, "Look how rosy she is!" Even now she inhabits the name with her whole being—she proclaims, "I am Rosie!" and all that the word entails is hers.

Although the girls inspire me with their firsts every day, my firsts tend to come less frequently as I get older, a fact that I am trying to remedy. Ricotta was the first cheese I made at home. When I witnessed the separation of curds and whey, I could not help but announce to my empty kitchen, "I'm a cheese maker!" There is a power in the transformation of milk that awes me every time, and the wonder of home cheese making draws new people into my kitchen every week.

"I just want to watch," they say.

"No! Have a quick stir! Make it yourself! I'll watch *you*!" I answer.

And with that, a new cheese maker is born.

Unlike many other homemade cheeses, ricotta requires neither cultures nor rennet. All you need is a half-gallon of milk and a lemon or two. The secret is to heat the milk slowly at a low temperature, stirring only a few times. Make it in the morning and use it in that night's lasagne, or just drizzle it with honey and eat it with a spoon.

RICOTTA MAKES ABOUT ¾ POUND (1½ CUPS)

- ½ gallon whole milk
- ⅓ cup fresh lemon juice (from 1½ to 2 lemons)
- *Optional:* ½ cup heavy cream
- *Optional:* salt (kosher or sea) to taste

1 Ice a large, heavy pot (see page 28). Add the milk and the lemon juice, and cream, if using, to the pot and stir without touching the bottom of the pot for 5 seconds.

2 Place the pot over low heat and attach a candy or cheese thermometer to the inside of the pot. Heat the milk mixture to 175°F. This should take 40 to 50 minutes, and you can stir once or twice over the course of this time.

3 Raise the heat to medium-high, and without stirring, watch the pot until the temperature reads 205°F, 3 to 5 minutes. The surface of the milk will look like it is about to erupt, but it shouldn't boil. Remove the pot from the heat and let sit for 10 minutes. Now you have curds and whey.

4 Lay a fine-meshed sieve over a large bowl or jar and line it with a double layer of damp cheesecloth. Using a large slotted spoon, scoop the curds into the cheesecloth. Let the cheese drain for 10 minutes, and if you like, sprinkle salt over the top of the curds.

storage
FRIDGE • covered container, 3 to 5 days
FREEZER • no

> **whey** ~ The cloudy liquid that separates from the curds is the whey. Don't throw it out! It's packed with nutrition, flavor, and protein. Use it instead of the milk or water in your Sandwich Bread (pages 212–214) or Cornbread (page 148) recipe, as an alternative to stock or water in the pureed soups (pages 134–136), and even in your smoothies in place of milk or juice. Whey keeps in the refrigerator for up to 2 weeks, and in the freezer, up to 6 months.

CRÈME FRAÎCHE IS JUST FANCY SOUR CREAM. I have a small wooden bowl that sits on the table and makes ordinary salt something special. On a hectic afternoon, I put cheap black tea into a pretty glass for Joey, and the tea becomes infused with class it would never have in an ordinary mug. It's all about what gets you through the day.

Joey and I became parents before we became adults, and such luxuries have made the daily craziness feel manageable, even enjoyable.

People say to me, "You're lucky to be parenting when you are young. Me? I never would have been ready at that age." You think we were ready? There is always a reason it's not time yet—a career to begin, money to save. We made that decision after a surprise positive pregnancy test, and most of our big decisions since then have been made in that same way, with a walk around the block together, a shrug, and the hope that we are in a moment of clarity.

Many of our friends moved to New York City to turn their majors into careers, but we're in the country, finding ways to live on less money than we ever thought possible. We make what we can, we try not to buy things we don't need, and we are creative about how to make our money last.

I have, however, had to come to terms with one truth. Like my younger daughter, who desires sparkles and loveliness around her, I am a bit of a princess. Fortunately, luxury does not necessarily require money. I have found small details that I can shift in our everyday existence to make life feel sumptuous and abundant. Cloth napkins. Flowers on the table (even if they are weeds from the backyard). Handfuls of fresh mint in a pitcher of tap water.

And crème fraîche on everything—from baked potatoes to apple pie to enchiladas. To say it is almost enough, but to taste it is even better.

CRÈME FRAÎCHE   MAKES 2 CUPS

- 1 pint heavy cream (not ultra-pasteurized)

- 3 tablespoons cultured Buttermilk, homemade (page 41) or store-bought, or 1 packet (½ teaspoon) crème fraîche culture (see page 30)

1 Pour the cream into a clean jar. Stir in the buttermilk or crème fraîche culture and set the lid on top of the jar without screwing it on.

2 Leave at room temperature for 16 to 24 hours, or until thickened. Refrigerate until you are ready to use.

storage

FRIDGE • covered container, 1 week

FREEZER • no

---

ice the pot ~ I have scorched the bottom of too many pots to count, but the day I spent in Ashfield, Massachusetts, with "the cheese queen," Ricki Carroll, changed it all. She showed me a simple trick to protect the pot while heating milk to high temperatures. Before you even turn on the stovetop, put an ice cube in the pot and move the pot around so the ice covers every inch of the bottom as it melts. When the ice is entirely melted, leave the cold water in the pot and just add the ingredients to it. As long as you don't touch a metal spoon to the bottom of the pot as you stir throughout the recipe, the milk won't scorch the bottom of the pot.

fOR ME, YOGURT WAS THE BEGINNING.

I had never thought about the power of making basic, everyday foods at home. I pondered puff pastry and roast chicken. Yogurt I happily ate out of plastic containers from the store.

One day I started thinking about all those plastic containers and the money I spent on them. Yogurt, one of the few nutritional foods that Rosie would eat, is at its highest nutritional content and best taste four to six days after its production. This was long before it ever got to my refrigerator. That Christmas, there was a yogurt maker with my name on it sitting under the tree.

The first time I left milk out to culture, it was a day of self-doubt. Wasn't I supposed to make sure that perishable food was refrigerated at all times? Was I really going to intentionally grow organisms in my clean milk? The companies that created my store-bought yogurt had done exactly that, but I trusted that they knew what they were doing. As the cultures worked on the milk in the yogurt maker, I watched my counter suspiciously, praying that I wouldn't poison my children with my selfish cooking experiments. But at the end of the day, I had creamy, perfect yogurt, and I never looked back.

Many people make yogurt with nothing but a mason jar and a warm spot in their kitchen, and that works just fine. I am partial to my yogurt maker, which is basically an electric mason jar.

YOGURT MAKES 5¼ CUPS

- 4½ cups whole milk (not ultra-pasteurized)
- 1½ teaspoons powdered yogurt starter (see below), or ½ cup plain unsweetened full-fat yogurt, preferably Greek

1 Ice a medium, heavy-bottomed pot (see page 28), and add the milk. Attach a candy or cheese thermometer to the inside of the pot and cook over medium heat until the milk hits 180°F, 15 to 20 minutes.

2 Remove the pot from the heat and let the milk cool to 110°F, either by letting it sit at room temperature or by putting the pot in a larger bowl or sink of ice water.

3 Empty the powdered starter or yogurt into a 4-cup liquid measuring cup. Add 1 cup of warm milk from the pot and whisk until fairly smooth. Add the mixture to the pot of warm milk and whisk until slightly foamy.

4 *If using a yogurt maker,* transfer half of the milk mixture back into the liquid measuring cup. Pour it into the individual cups of your yogurt maker. Refill the measuring cup with the remaining mixture in the pot and fill the rest of the containers, covering them according to the yogurt maker instructions. *If using mason jars,* fill a large and a small jar with the mixture and screw on the lids. Wrap the jars in a towel to keep them warm and place them in an insulated cooler.

recipe continues

---

what is a starter? ~ In any recipe where you are culturing your ingredients, you need specific bacteria to do the work; the bacteria are the starter. For yogurt, I prefer powdered starter, but different kinds are available, and each will produce a different flavored and textured yogurt. The extra yogurt you set aside will serve as your starter for the next batch. As you continue to do this, in five to eight times the bacteria will get weaker, and the yogurt won't firm up. Then make a batch with new starter. If you don't have access to a powdered starter, you can use store-bought yogurt as long as it's not past its expiration date.

New England Cheese Making Supply (www.cheesemaking.com) has a great supply of yogurt, cheese, buttermilk, and crème fraîche starters.

variations ~

- **FLAVORED YOGURT** Plain yogurt can be topped with jam, honey, or maple syrup, but you can also experiment with flavors in your yogurt. Here are a few of my favorites. Remember that you need plain, unsweetened yogurt to use for your next batch, so when you make flavored yogurt, make sure to reserve some plain milk to make your starter.

- **FRUIT ON THE BOTTOM** Use only $3\frac{1}{2}$ cups milk. Bring $1\frac{1}{2}$ cups Jam (page 84) to a boil in a small saucepan, then let cool to 110°F. Spoon a scant $\frac{1}{4}$ cup of warm jam into each container (or all the jam into the mason jar). Top with the milk/culture mixture and continue as directed.

- **CHOCOLATE** Combine $\frac{1}{2}$ cup unsweetened cocoa powder and 3 tablespoons sugar in a small bowl. Whisk into the hot milk in the big pot and cool to 110°F. Continue as directed.

- **COFFEE** Combine 2 tablespoons instant espresso powder or 3 tablespoons instant coffee with 3 tablespoons sugar in a small bowl. Whisk into the hot milk in the big pot and cool to 110°F. Continue as directed.

- **MAPLE** Whisk $\frac{1}{3}$ cup maple syrup into the hot milk in the big pot and cool to 110°F. Continue as directed.

5   Wait 5 hours, then check to make sure the yogurt is firm. If not, let the yogurt culture for 1 to 2 more hours. Remove the containers from the yogurt maker or insulated cooler. Cover and refrigerate for 2 hours before serving. Set one yogurt container or the small mason jar aside to serve as the starter for your next batch.

storage

FRIDGE • covered container, 2 weeks (discard when mold grows on the surface)

FREEZER • no

---

tense moments ~

THE YOGURT DOES NOT FIRM UP AND IT SMELLS MORE LIKE PLAIN OR SOUR MILK This means the cultures were not active. Try a new starter and start over for a batch that will be protected by live cultures as it sits out.

THE YOGURT IS RUNNY Be sure your milk is not ultra-pasteurized. If it has been heated too much in the past, it won't respond to the cultures. Your starter yogurt could also be a little weak. You can use the runny yogurt in dressings and smoothies—it is safe to eat. If your yogurt is consistently runnier than you prefer, add a few tablespoons of nonfat dry milk powder to the starter, and that will firm up the texture.

THERE IS WATER IN MY YOGURT, ON THE TOP OR BOTTOM OF THE CONTAINER This is whey, and it is an indicator that your yogurt cultured too long. It is fine to eat, but next time try letting it sit for 1 hour less.

MY STARTER IS ONLY LASTING THROUGH ONE OR TWO GENERATIONS OF YOGURT, OR MY YOGURT IS BECOMING MOLDY TOO FAST Make sure that all of your tools and containers are clean; otherwise, you are introducing other bacteria into the situation. This will weaken the good bacteria in your starter—and the starter won't work as well, or the yogurt will spoil faster. If you continue to have this problem, sterilize your tools and containers (in a hot dishwasher or 10 minutes in boiling water) before you make yogurt.

MY YOGURT DOESN'T TASTE GOOD Whether you are using powdered starter or store-bought yogurt, different starters will change the taste and consistency of your yogurt. Next time, try a different starter.

a S YOU STRETCH CHEESE CURDS in your own kitchen, mozzarella can become your new superpower. Homemade mozzarella costs less than store-bought, and it tastes better. When I add rennet to the heated milk and watch the curds take shape, I am in awe. When the curds are strong enough to knead, I am invincible. When the curds stretch without breaking, I am super-me. When I am slicing my own mozzarella on family pizza night, nothing can bring me down.

This is my take on the 30-Minute Mozzarella recipe (*Home Cheese Making*, Storey, 2002) from Ricki Carroll, the queen of home cheese making. She has been teaching people to make cheese at her home in Ashfield, Massachusetts, since 1978, and her easy mozzarella has turned thousands of people into cheese makers.

Making mozzarella is a three-step process. First, the milk and acid are heated together in order to separate the curds from whey, just like for Ricotta (page 26). Then we make that curd stronger and more solid by adding both rennet and heat. We also cut the curd into cubes so they can heat faster and more thoroughly, and so there is more surface area from which the curd can release whey as it heats. Finally, the curds are removed, the whey is heated even more, and the strong curds are resubmerged in the hot whey until they are warm enough to stretch. Stretching and folding the curd gets rid of any whey that might be left, and the result is smooth and glossy mozzarella.

Homemade mozzarella is heavenly on its own, but feel free to bring in additions that inspire you. I love to roll the warm balls of cheese in fresh herbs or thinly sliced prosciutto.

MOZZARELLA MAKES 1 POUND

- 1½ teaspoons citric acid (see page 35)
- 1¼ cups cool water (filtered or boiled)
- 1 gallon whole milk (not ultra-pasteurized)
- ⅓ teaspoon liquid rennet (see page 35)
- 4 tablespoons kosher salt

1. Ice a large, heavy pot (see page 28). Combine the citric acid with 1 cup of the water in a 2-cup liquid measuring cup. Add the milk to the pot. Slowly pour the citric acid mixture into the milk, gently stirring with a slotted spoon for 15 seconds. Set the pot over medium heat, attach a cheese or candy thermometer to the pot, and heat the milk to 90°F, stirring every 2 to 3 minutes. This will take about 10 minutes, and the milk will start to curdle. Remove the pot from heat.

2. Combine the rennet with the remaining ¼ cup water in the liquid measure. Pour the rennet mixture into the milk, and gently stir with a scooping motion for 30 seconds. Cover the pot and let sit for 5 minutes. The curds will solidify into one mass that looks like tofu or custard. Press your finger about ½ inch into the curd. If it comes out mostly clean, the curd is ready to cut. Otherwise, check again in 2 minutes.

3. With the curd still in the pot, cut it into 2-inch cubes: place a long knife 2 inches from the left side of the pot and draw it through the curd toward you in a straight line, taking care to cut to the bottom of the curd. Continue with parallel lines to the first in 2-inch increments. Turn the pot 90°, and repeat so that you have a grid. Then, make 2-inch diagonal cuts at a 45° angle to the side of the pot. Repeat from the other side. Cubes of curd will float in the whey.

4. Return the pot to medium heat and stir the curds very gently with a slotted spoon as you heat the whey to 110°F. Remove from the heat. Set a metal colander over the mixing bowl and use the spoon to gently transfer only the curds into the colander. Set the curds aside.

5. Return the pot with the whey to medium-high heat. Add the salt and heat until the whey reaches 170°F, about 10 minutes. If there is any whey in the mixing bowl, add it to the pot. Reduce the heat to medium to keep the whey between 165°F and 180°F for the next step.

recipe continues

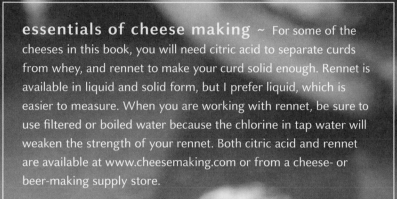

essentials of cheese making ~ For some of the cheeses in this book, you will need citric acid to separate curds from whey, and rennet to make your curd solid enough. Rennet is available in liquid and solid form, but I prefer liquid, which is easier to measure. When you are working with rennet, be sure to use filtered or boiled water because the chlorine in tap water will weaken the strength of your rennet. Both citric acid and rennet are available at www.cheesemaking.com or from a cheese- or beer-making supply store.

6   Transfer half the curds to a medium mixing bowl and set them aside. Submerge the colander with the remaining curds into the hot whey until they get glossy, about 1 minute. Put on heatproof rubber gloves to pick up the curds and firmly squeeze them into a ball over the pot. The ball will release more whey as you squeeze. Put the ball back into the hot whey for 1 minute, then stretch it between your hands, folding it back on itself. Put the cheese into the whey again and repeat the process up to three times, until the cheese is soft and glossy and holds together as you stretch it up to 12 inches. The surface of the cheese should be smooth. When you have reached this consistency, you can eat the mozzarella warm, dividing it into little balls if you'd like. Repeat the heating and stretching process with the second half of the curd.

7   If you would like to store the cheese, put the balls in a bowl, cover with cool water, and let sit for 5 minutes. Then add ice cubes and keep the mozzarella there for 30 minutes. Remove the cheese from the water and transfer into a covered container.

storage

FRIDGE · covered container, 4 days
FREEZER · no

---

tense moments ~ It is possible that your curds will be weak and you won't achieve a clean break when you test it with your finger. The culprit for this problem is most likely your milk. Mozzarella will not work with milk that has been ultra-pasteurized (heated to 275°F or higher). Sometimes even pasteurized milk has been heated to a higher temperature. So if you are having trouble getting a strong curd, strain it and use it like ricotta, and next time try another brand of milk. Local milk tends to be heated to a lower temperature because it does not have to travel far, and raw milk is not heated at all. For a list of safe milks for cheese making, you can visit www.cheesemaking.com.

hALFWAY THROUGH KINDERGARTEN, two boys cornered Sadie on the playground and told her she was fat. Oh, beware the rage of a mother who is protecting her daughter's body image! I was angry with the boys, and angrier with their mothers. Where would a young boy get the idea that all women should be one particular shape?

In the following weeks, Sadie would spontaneously exclaim how fat she was. Her sister joined in, pointing to her belly with theatrical disdain. I was heartbroken and at a total loss as to what to do.

I hail from a family of small Jewish women with large breasts, skinny legs, and round bellies. My grandmother tortured herself at Weight Watchers in her final years, trying to shrink the portly tummy that made her feel undesirable. She passed her shape to my mother, who worked tirelessly to defy her genetics, and she in turn passed it to me. I have lost patience with this obsession with thinness and have declared that in my house, a round belly is a thing of great beauty.

In the end, the solution was to focus on the messages that we have stuck with all along. Play outside, eat good food, and our bodies will find the shape that suits them. Sadie's anxiety eased, and I relaxed. A few weeks later, Sadie came home asking why her friend's mother told her butter was bad for her figure. I know these messages will come in waves. Nevertheless, I am determined to raise girls who are not afraid of butter.

Unless you have a dairy cow in your backyard (oh, if only!), butter costs less to buy at the store than it does to make at home, so for cooking and baking, I buy my butter.

However, when it comes to toast, homemade butter is the ultimate treat. The flavor of the cream comes through in astounding ways, and fresh butter tastes like sun and air and grass. The girls roll their butter between sheets of waxed paper so they can cut hearts and stars with cookie cutters. I love to mix soft butters with herbs, nasturtium petals, or chopped shallots, adding a squeeze of lemon juice and salt to taste.

BUTTER   MAKES 6 TO 8 OUNCES (12 TO 16 TABLESPOONS)

- 1 pint heavy cream
- ½ teaspoon kosher salt

1 Combine the cream and salt in the bowl of a stand mixer fitted with the paddle attachment and cover with a dish towel to prevent splattering. Beat at medium to high speed, peeking in every 20 seconds or so. In 1 to 3 minutes, the cream will be whipped and airy, then it will stiffen. After that, the cream will break, and you will have both liquids and solids in the bowl.

2 When the fat separates from the buttermilk, pour the buttermilk into a jar and refrigerate to use within 3 days. (It will make remarkable Pancakes, page 144.)

3 Run your hands under cold water, then squeeze the butter together, kneading it in the bowl. Place the bowl in the sink, rinse the butter in cold water, and squeeze it again. Repeat this process until the water runs clear and the butter does not release any liquid when you press on it.

storage
ROOM TEMPERATURE • covered container or butter bell, 5 days
FRIDGE • covered container, 1 week
FREEZER • roll and cut into sticks, wrap individually in plastic wrap and a freezer bag, 3 months

---

tense moments ~ Don't skimp on the squeezing and kneading of the butter—if you do, the buttermilk still trapped in your butter will cause the butter to go rancid within a day! So keep kneading until there is no sign of cloudy buttermilk coming out of the butter.

I DIDN'T HAVE A CLUE about buttermilk until recently, and I didn't know what it was for. I substituted milk for buttermilk in baking recipes, determined not to buy an ingredient that I would use only for one thing and then throw out when it went (even more) sour.

Buttermilk is now one of the most important ingredients in my refrigerator. Like anchovies, good olive oil, and decent Parmesan cheese, buttermilk can transform an ordinary thrown-together supper into something wonderful. Baked goods with buttermilk taste better and rise more effectively, and any left over will be the base for the most delicious salad dressing.

"Buttermilk" can refer to two entirely different liquids, and both can be made at home. The first, the liquid by-product of the butter-making process (see page 39), is a precious substance to use in your pancake and baking recipes. This delicious milky liquid is the buttermilk of times past, and is only available to those who make a batch of butter at home.

The second is cultured buttermilk, and this is what we are making here. Like Yogurt (page 30) and Crème Fraîche (page 28), it is simply milk combined with a culture, and it is similar to what you will find today in the dairy section of your supermarket. It is also useful in pancakes and baked goods, and cultured buttermilk is what you need for dressings and cultured Crème Fraîche.

BUTTERMILK MAKES 1 QUART

1 Attach a cheese or candy thermometer to the inside of a medium saucepan. Pour in the milk and cook over medium heat until it reaches 72°F on the thermometer, 3 to 5 minutes.

2 Stir in the buttermilk culture, transfer to a clean jar, and set the lid on top of the jar without screwing it on top.

3 Let sit at room temperature for 12 to 16 hours, until thickened. Refrigerate until ready to use.

- 1 quart whole milk (not ultra-pasteurized)
- 1 packet (½ teaspoon) buttermilk culture (see page 30)

storage

FRIDGE • covered container, 7 to 10 days

FREEZER • 1-cup portions in freezer-safe containers, 4 months (thaw in refrigerator and shake before using)

---

quick buttermilk ~ Need buttermilk now? Combine 1 cup milk and 1½ tablespoons of lemon juice, stir, and let sit for 5 minutes. This will work for any baking recipe that requires buttermilk for its leavening capabilities. For sauces and dressings, and for culturing Crème Fraîche (page 28), you need cultured buttermilk.

CREAM CHEESE

—or—

rosie's soul food

tHERE IS A COUCH IN MY KITCHEN, and it is my favorite place in the house. Kitchens are for cooking, eating, and talking—and for this we need a few appliances, a brief length of counter, a table, and a place to recline.

A couch in the kitchen performs several functions: it's a resting spot during a foolishly attempted 48-hour-long recipe; a comfy seat for those who love to watch others cook; or a surface on which to stack cookbooks, however precariously. Our kitchen couch has a new identity, and we have named it "the couch of refusal." Many nights, this is where Rosie spends most of dinnertime.

Here's how it goes. There is cooking and shuffling of dishes and pouring of water and milk, and a holler from me, "Dinner! Come and set the table!" (I never thought I would be so traditional in this regard, but here I am, with an apron around my waist and a large wooden spoon in my hand.) Rosie is usually the first to trot in, and she eyes the counter critically. She puckers her lips for a kiss, and after receiving one, unless dinner is bread or noodles or popovers, meows the same phrase: "I hate what's for dinner."

All my food love will not get this girl to cheer at the dinner menu. I say something like, "Well, honey, that's what's for dinner," which is, like clockwork, followed by crossed arms and four words: "Cream cheese and jelly."

I will not serve my daughter cream cheese and jelly for dinner—because she had it for breakfast, lunch, and a mid-afternoon snack as well. So she takes her grumpy perch on the couch. I don't know what eventually gets her off the couch, but she usually takes her seat with us by the end of the meal.

In my best moments, I know that many children have gone on to live long and healthy lives after years of toast and buttered noodles, and that Rosie will someday expand her repertoire. But for now, we go through a lot of cream cheese around here.

CREAM CHEESE   MAKES JUST UNDER 1 POUND (1½ CUPS)

1 Attach a cheese or candy thermometer to the side of a medium saucepan that you can do without for a day. Add the cream and milk to the saucepan and warm over medium heat until it reaches 70°F.

2 Sprinkle in the starter and let sit for 1 minute. Add the diluted rennet. Mix thoroughly, cover, and let sit undisturbed at room temperature for 10 to 12 hours, or until the mixture resembles very firm yogurt. If the room is colder than 72°F, wrap the pot in towels and place it into a cooler to keep it warm.

3 Line a fine-meshed sieve with a large enough piece of cheesecloth that you can tie the ends together in a little sack. Set the sieve into your sink.

4 Gently pour the curds through the sieve, discarding the liquid that drains through. Tie the corners of the cloth together and hang to drain until the sack stops dripping entirely, 8 to 10 hours. You can tie the sack around your faucet (if your family won't complain too much about having a bag of cream cheese in your sink), or you can hang it in another location with a bowl below it to catch the drips (away from your pets!). Open the sack, place the cream cheese in a container, and mix with salt, herbs, or whatever your pleasure.

storage
FRIDGE · covered container, 1 week

FREEZER · no

- 2 cups heavy cream (not ultra-pasteurized)
- 2 cups whole milk (not ultra-pasteurized)
- 1 packet (½ teaspoon) direct-set mesophilic starter (see page 30)
- 1 drop liquid rennet (see page 35), diluted in ¼ cup filtered or boiled water
- *Optional:* kosher salt, fresh herbs, horseradish, honey, or whatever inspires you!

granola

instant oatmeal

popcorn

buttered popcorn

maple popcorn

toaster pastries

car snacks

the cereal bar

the sweet bar

the nutty granola bar

potato chips

mixed roasted nuts

jerky

fOLD DOWN THIS PAGE. You are going to want to come back to this recipe a lot. If you are going to ditch one packaged thing from your pantry, I suggest the cereal box. In its place comes granola, one of the easiest and most gratifying foods you can create yourself.

In my family, granola is an all-day kind of food. There is the morning bowl with milk or yogurt, then there is the panicked and hungry afternoon handful, and most important, the nighttime dessert after the kids are long asleep, maybe with a squeeze of honey if it has been a hard night. Once you start making granola, it will always be there for you.

The first few times you make this recipe, you might think of it as mine. You can follow each ingredient to the letter, and it will be like any good and usable recipe in any other cookbook on your shelf. But think of this recipe as a template for your own perfect bowl. It could start with a note or two in the margin, noting this or that addition or adjustment. You might even find entirely new combinations tailored to your very own liking. Before you know it, you'll be referring to it as "my granola," and people will be asking for your secret recipe. That's good! What starts as mine will hopefully become yours, and then you should take all the credit. It may seem like a lot of granola, but I predict the jar will be empty before the end of the week.

GRANOLA   MAKES 3½ POUNDS (ABOUT 16 CUPS)

- 10 cups (2 pounds) old-fashioned rolled oats
- ¾ cup (3.75 ounces) sesame seeds
- ½ cup (2.5 ounces) sunflower seeds
- 2 cups (6 ounces) raw sliced or roughly chopped almonds
- 1 cup (2.5 ounces) shredded unsweetened coconut
- ½ teaspoon kosher salt
- 1½ tablespoons ground cinnamon
- ¾ cup canola oil
- 1 cup maple syrup
- 1½ tablespoons Vanilla Extract, homemade (page 165) or store-bought
- 1½ teaspoons almond extract
- *Optional:* ¼ cup Lyle's Golden Syrup (see page 63), dried fruit

1   Preheat the oven to 250°F. Position both racks in the upper two-thirds of the oven.

2   Combine the oats, sesame seeds, sunflower seeds, almonds, coconut, salt, and cinnamon in your largest bowl. Stir until the contents are uniformly mixed. In a 4-cup liquid measuring cup, whisk together the oil, maple syrup, vanilla, almond extract, and golden syrup, if using, to make a uniform syrup. Pour this mixture into the bowl. Stir until everything is coated and there are no hidden pockets of syrup or dry ingredients in your bowl.

3   Line two 18 × 13-inch jelly-roll pans with parchment paper. Spread the granola in an even layer on each pan. Put them in the oven and set your timer for 30 minutes. Clean up the kitchen. Then shuffle the granola and switch the trays and rotate them. Go do something else for another 30 minutes. Then shuffle, switch, and rotate again. Set the timer for the last 30 minutes. Now do something really lovely for yourself. After all, you've just made your own granola!

4   At the end of the full 90 minutes of baking, turn off the oven, but leave the granola there for up to 6 hours. It will harden and crisp up as the oven cools. If you like raisins or other dried fruit in your granola, sprinkle them over the top of the granola just before eating.

storage
ROOM TEMPERATURE • covered container, 3 weeks
FREEZER • freezer-safe container or bag, 6 months (thaw at room temperature)

WHEN IT COMES TO MOTHERING, I do my best. I make the occasional post-school plate of cookies, I take the girls for walks in the woods, and I say yes whenever I can. I don't play so much, but I married a man who does. I'm not a yeller, and although clothes are not usually new, they are almost always in the desired color of the moment. I'm a pretty good mom . . . unless it's before 8:00 A.M.

Joey and I have made several attempts over the years at proving that parenthood doesn't require early rising. When Sadie was two, we left her a bowl of dry cereal on the shelf at night and a tiny pitcher of milk in the refrigerator. That routine lasted a week, and then she lost interest and stomped through the bedroom again with claims of "tarving!"

When Rosie and Sadie hit ages five and seven, respectively, the longstanding don't-wake-up-mommy-and-daddy-until-8:00-on-the-weekends rule went from laughable joke to respected law. The house became a secret place before we stumbled into the kitchen; they create whole worlds in that time—stores to buy and sell paper ice-cream cones, orphanages with mean owners who make them sweep the kitchen, and (on the very best days!) restaurants to serve their sleepy parents breakfast in bed.

To aid in the continued success of these weekend mornings, I do my best to supply plenty of breakfast options they can serve themselves. There is, of course, granola, toast with jam, and yogurt with honey. But the real winner is instant oatmeal.

There is something so enticing about the single-serving, just-add-water model. It certainly got me through a lot of mornings as a kid. When I found the right homemade mixture, I put it in a big container with a sign that directs the girls to the right proportions. Sadie starts the electric teakettle, scoops out the oatmeal for her and her sister, and I get at least another hour in bed.

INSTANT OATMEAL

1 Preheat the oven to 325°F. Spread the oats on a baking sheet and bake for 20 minutes. Cool slightly.

2 In the bowl of a food processor, combine 4 cups of the toasted oats, the brown sugar, cinnamon, and salt. Pulse until the mixture is a rough powder.

3 Pour into a large wide-mouthed jar or container. Pour in the remaining 2 cups of oats and the fruit, if using. Stir thoroughly and top with the lid.

4 To make the oatmeal, combine ½ cup of the mixture with 1 to 1½ cups boiling water. Cover with a plate and let sit for 5 minutes before stirring and serving.

- 6 cups (1 pound, 3 ounces) old-fashioned rolled oats
- ½ cup (4 ounces) packed light brown sugar, homemade (see below) or store-bought, or more or less to taste
- 1 tablespoon ground cinnamon
- 1 teaspoon salt
- *Optional:* dried or dehydrated fruit

storage

ROOM TEMPERATURE • covered container, 4 weeks

FRIDGE • covered container, 3 months

FREEZER • freezer-safe container or bag, 6 months

---

make your own brown sugar! ~ Combine 1 cup granulated sugar with 2 teaspoons unsulphured molasses. Fluff with a fork or beat in a stand mixer until the molasses is entirely incorporated in the sugar. There will be a tense moment—the molasses will clump—but carry on! Mix a bit more and you will have brown sugar. For darker brown sugar, increase your molasses. Store in a covered container for up to 6 months.

POPCORN

–or–

the magic machine

mY GRANDPARENTS HAD AN AIR POPPER they would pull out for me on the best Saturday afternoons—the same machine that they used when my mother was young. The popper would spark as soon as the plug touched the outlet, and I would cheer with the commencement of its deafening whir.

Although many have tried to convert me to popping corn in an oily pot, I have never succumbed. I have also tried to embrace microwave popcorn for its warmth and convenience, but the bag was off-putting. (How does heating that material to a high temperature seem like a good idea?) When I had children, I searched for an air popper so I could carry on the line, and as I perused the shelves of my local hardware store, I was surprised to find a less dusty version of the very same machine I had known throughout my childhood. It seems after all that such a perfect invention leaves no room for improvement, and that the introductory spark upon plugging in is a necessary step in making the best popcorn.

An air popper can fill a bored and hungry afternoon with something warm and homemade in just a few minutes. To say "Popcorn?" with the right intonation will snap my girls out of the worst of moods, and the sight of the corn bursting out of the mouth of the popper never fails to strike Rosie as entirely hilarious—at the first pop she falls off her stool with the force of her own laughter.

Popcorn is also an excellent option for a savory snack, even a whole-grain one. We usually pour a touch of melted butter and salt over the popped corn and that is that. For those of you with a sweet tooth, my friend Michele DiSimone, mama to three who are never bored or hungry, has shared her Maple Popcorn recipe (page 54). It makes a big batch, but beware—it will be gone before you know it. It also makes a great gift.

BUTTERED POPCORN MAKES 8 CUPS

1 *If you are using an air popper,* use according to the machine's instructions. *If using a pot,* heat the oil over medium-high heat. Add a few kernels to the pot and cover. When the kernels pop, remove from heat, add the remaining kernels and ½ teaspoon salt, and cover the pot. Count to ten. Shift the lid so there is a crack to let steam escape, return the pot to medium-high heat, and shake it gently over the heat as the kernels start to pop.

2 When all the kernels are popped, pour the popcorn into a bowl and mix first with melted butter, then with flavorings, if using.

storage
ROOM TEMPERATURE • covered container, 3 days
FREEZER • no

- ½ cup unpopped popcorn
- Salt, to taste
- 4 tablespoons olive oil or canola oil (if you are popping the corn in a pot)
- 2 tablespoons unsalted butter, melted
- *Optional flavorings:* dried sage, dried dill, ground cumin, chili powder, smoked paprika, nutritional yeast (see note)

not baker's yeast! ~ Nutritional yeast is a flaky, yellow, inactive yeast found at any health food or gourmet store, often in the bulk department. It is packed with vitamin B_{12}, high in protein, and has a wonderful cheesy flavor that makes it an addictive and satisfying addition to popcorn.

MAPLE POPCORN MAKES 18 CUPS

- 1 cup (8 ounces) unsalted butter, plus additional to butter the bowl and pans
- 1 cup unpopped popcorn
- 1 cup maple syrup
- ¾ cup raw sugar
- 1 teaspoon salt
- ½ teaspoon baking soda
- 1 teaspoon Vanilla Extract, homemade (page 165) or store-bought

1 Preheat the oven to 250°F. Butter two 9 × 13-inch baking pans and your largest bowl.

2 Pop the corn according to your preference (see page 53) and transfer the popcorn to the buttered bowl.

3 In a medium saucepan, melt the butter with the maple syrup, sugar, and salt. Bring to a boil over medium-high heat and let it cook, without stirring, for 5 minutes. Add the baking soda and vanilla and stir to combine. The mixture will foam up and bubble and smoke.

4 Very gently (or your popcorn might deflate!), pour 1 cup of the sugar mixture over the popped corn and stir until evenly coated. Coat with more sugar mixture and stir again, repeating until all of the sugar mixture is coating the popcorn. Divide the popcorn between the two baking pans.

5 Bake for 1 hour, stirring the popcorn every 15 minutes. Cool before serving.

storage

ROOM TEMPERATURE • covered container, 3 weeks

FREEZER • freezer-safe container or bag, 6 months (great right out of the freezer)

I HAVE A FEW RECIPES that emerged out of maternal guilt. The spring I pulled my first toaster pastries out of the oven, I had recently left my job to start writing full time, and it was beginning to seem like I would find balance between work and everything else. I went to a rally to support our library, and in moments, everything changed. A friend reminded me of the upcoming local election. "There are no good candidates!" she complained with a sideways glance. Before I could blink, there were signs with my name on them all over town, and I was shopping for a few more button-down shirts.

I was eventually elected selectman, a member of the governing body of the town. It was quite a time leading up to that election, and most days I talked to the local paper, public access channel, or anyone on the street who just had to ask: "Why did you decide to get involved in local government?"

The answer always came down to "my kids." And if you expand your view beyond just me, you will see those very kids, pulling on my skirt, tired, sick of listening to Mommy talk about local government—kids who just want to go to the library and have me all to themselves. I felt torn, split between wanting to make things better for their community and just being with them. Throughout the campaign, no matter how much praise I got for my self-sacrificing ways, I had more bad mother moments than I care to recount. And it was then that I tried to re-create the toaster pastry.

I was never allowed to eat those sweet treats as a child, but I certainly dreamed about them. These homemade versions ended up better than the few boxed ones that I eventually got my hands on. Mine were flaky and warm like the best pie for breakfast. Even more, pulling them out of the oven for the girls did the trick. Something that lovely in the morning can only taste like an apology, and with an extra sifting of powdered sugar, the girls cheered, and I went a little easier on myself.

TOASTER PASTRIES MAKES 6 PASTRIES

- **One recipe Basic Pie Crust** (page 150)
- **Flour for the counter**
- **1 large egg, beaten with 1 tablespoon of water**
- **6 tablespoons filling of choice (see page 59)**
- *Optional:* **powdered sugar, Best Frosting (page 157)**

1 Prepare the pie crust in two discs according to the recipe and refrigerate for at least 2 hours but up to 2 days.

2 Preheat the oven to 375°F. Line a baking sheet with parchment paper.

3 Roll the first disc of pie pastry on a lightly floured surface into a 9 × 12-inch rectangle, cutting away any errant edges with a sharp knife.

4 Cut the rectangle into six smaller rectangles. Gently separate the rectangles from the counter and lay them on the prepared baking sheet with at least 2 inches between them.

5 With a pastry brush, paint each rectangle with the beaten egg. You will have some egg mixture left—set it aside.

6 Scoop 1 tablespoon of filling onto each rectangle in a thin line down the center. Roll out the second disc of pie pastry, repeating the steps to create six rectangles.

7 Lay the new batch of rectangles over the rectangles with filling and seal by pressing a fork around the perimeter of each rectangle. Using the pastry brush, paint the tops of each pastry with egg wash and poke several times with a fork.

8 Bake for 20 to 25 minutes, or until golden. Cool on a wire rack for at least 20 minutes before dusting with powdered sugar or spreading with frosting.

storage

FRIDGE • covered container, 3 days (reheat in a toaster or 375°F oven for 5 minutes)

FREEZER • freeze unbaked in single layers on parchment paper–lined baking sheet and transfer to freezer-safe container with layers of parchment (bake when ready to serve)

sweet fillings

- **JAM** (page 84) The classic.
- **NUTELLA** If you happen to have a jar around.
- **CINNAMON AND SUGAR** Mix 2 tablespoons cinnamon with 5 table-spoons sugar.

savory fillings

- **PESTO** (page 197) **AND RICOTTA** (page 26) A toaster pastry worthy of a cocktail party.
- **TOMATO SAUCE** (page 195) **AND CHEESE** Make your own pizza pockets.
- **POTATO** Combine leftover mashed potatoes with sautéed onions, sprinkle the top of the pastry with sesame seeds.

CAR SNACKS

—or—

the most important meal of the day

WHEN SADIE WAS BORN, she took in the entire room with full comprehension, looking at each person over the expanse of the nose that dominated her face. I loved her immediately, and I knew I was in for it.

Sadie talked at nine months and quickly moved to full conversations. When her little sister was born a few months shy of her second birthday, Sadie wrote a poem to commemorate the occasion. To this day she weighs in on every single thing. Thank God for Sadie. She keeps us all honest and fair.

Sadie was the one who explained the importance of the car snack. It did not work for her to wait to eat until she got home from school, and she was clear that I better find a way to feed her before then. Otherwise, there would be tears and screams and other sounds that make driving difficult.

For a few years I bought any bar that came six to a box so I could shove it in their lunchboxes. The girls would attack them with delight and throw the wrappers on the floor. One day I noticed Rosie making princess crowns in the backseat from empty granola bar packages. Holding her head still to keep the foil crown steady, she exclaimed, "I am the wrapper princess!" It was time to make a change.

I have tried to sneak a lot of failed recipes into the girls' lunchboxes—grains bound by sweetness that fall apart before they even reach the mouth or delicious concoctions that have to be chipped out of the pan with a chisel. But my car-snack battles have won me three excellent options: a crispy rice treat with fruit and chocolate, an oat square with sweetness and crunch, and the classic nutty granola bar.

I also turn into a bit of a hungry monster at 3:00, so I carry one of these around in my bag. Call it a work snack, a hiking snack, or a subway snack, but just make sure you don't leave the kitchen without at least one.

CAR SNACK 1 (THE CEREAL BAR)

MAKES SIXTEEN 2¼ × 3¼-INCH BARS

- ¼ cup canola oil, plus additional for greasing the dish
- 1½ cups (4.75 ounces) old-fashioned rolled oats
- 1½ cups (.75 ounce) puffed millet (or puffed rice cereal)
- 1½ cups loosely packed chopped dried fruit
- 1½ cups (4.5 ounces) toasted sliced almonds
- 1 tablespoon ground cinnamon
- ½ teaspoon kosher salt
- ¾ cup (4.5 ounces) semisweet chocolate chips
- ½ cup brown rice syrup (available at health food stores)
- ¼ cup (2 ounces) packed light brown sugar, homemade (page 51) or store-bought
- 1 tablespoon Vanilla Extract, homemade (page 165) or store-bought

THIS IS FOR THE CRISPY RICE TREAT folks who don't mind a little puffed millet in the backseat of their car now and then. It comes together in just a few minutes, and requires no baking.

1 Lightly grease a 9 × 13-inch baking dish. In a medium mixing bowl, combine the oats, puffed millet, dried fruit, almonds, cinnamon, salt, and chocolate chips.

2 In a medium saucepan, combine the brown rice syrup, brown sugar, oil, and vanilla. Stir frequently over medium-high heat, until 1 minute past boiling. Pour the syrup over the mixture in the bowl and coat thoroughly.

3 Spread the mixture into the prepared pan, press down with a spatula, and refrigerate for 1 hour. Cut into bars as you are ready to eat or pack them.

storage

FRIDGE • in covered pan, 10 days

FREEZER • wrap individual bars in plastic wrap and store together in freezer bag, 4 months

CAR SNACK 2 (THE SWEET BAR)

MAKES TWELVE 2 × 2¼-INCH BARS

THIS BAR IS A VARIATION on the British flapjack. It is a tea-time kind of snack, all crunch and caramel.

1   Preheat the oven to 350°F. Line an 8- or 9-inch square baking pan with parchment paper, leaving extra paper for pulling the finished product out of the pan.

2   Combine the butter, brown sugar, and syrup in the saucepan, and heat over medium heat until melted, about 3 minutes. Add the oats, salt, and almonds to the mixture and coat thoroughly. Transfer to the prepared pan and pat down with a spatula.

3   Bake until the edges darken, about 25 minutes. The mixture will be soft when you take it out of the oven, but allow it to cool completely before taking it out of the pan and cutting into 12 squares.

storage

ROOM TEMPERATURE • in covered pan, 10 days (or individually wrapped for convenience)

FREEZER • wrap individual bars in plastic wrap and store together in freezer bag, 4 months

- ½ cup (1 stick) unsalted butter
- ½ cup (4 ounces) packed light brown sugar, homemade (page 51) or store-bought
- ½ cup Lyle's Golden Syrup (see below)
- 2 cups (6.35 ounces) old-fashioned rolled oats
- ½ teaspoon kosher salt
- 1 cup (3 ounces) raw sliced almonds

---

what is lyle's golden syrup? ~ Golden syrup is a British sugar syrup that is becoming more popular in the United States owing to its wonderful flavor and ability to replace corn syrup. I use golden syrup in many of my recipes, but if you have trouble finding it, you can replace the golden syrup with corn syrup in recipes that require the consistency of golden syrup, such as Marshmallows (page 274) and Caramels (page 260). When golden syrup is used purely for its flavor, as in The Sweet Bar and Granola (page 48), honey can also be used.

CAR SNACK 3 (THE NUTTY GRANOLA BAR)

MAKES SIXTEEN 2¼ × 3¼-INCH BARS

- ¼ cup (½ stick) unsalted butter
- ¼ cup (2 ounces) coconut oil (or butter)
- ¾ cup Nut Butter, homemade (page 121) or store-bought
- ½ cup (4 ounces) packed light brown sugar, homemade (page 51) or store-bought
- 2 tablespoons Vanilla Extract, homemade (page 165) or store-bought
- ⅓ cup honey
- 2½ cups (8 ounces) old-fashioned rolled oats
- 1½ cups (4.5 ounces) raw sliced almonds
- ½ cup (1.25 ounces) shredded unsweetened coconut
- ¾ cup (4.5 ounces) semisweet chocolate chips
- ½ cup (2 ounces) oat bran (or ½ cup old-fashioned rolled oats ground to a powder in the blender or food processor)
- ¼ cup (1.25 ounces) sesame seeds
- ½ teaspoon ground cinnamon
- ½ teaspoon kosher salt

THIS BAR ACTUALLY TASTES EVEN BETTER than those classic packaged granola bars that I love, and it's filled with all sorts of things to help you get through a long day. I give endless thanks to my friend Meg Eisenhauer Barry for solving this puzzle. Although there are a lot of ingredients, putting the bars together takes only a few minutes. If you, too, have been searching for *the* granola bar, try this one.

1   Preheat the oven to 350°F. Line a 9 × 13-inch baking pan with parchment paper, leaving extra paper to pull the finished product out of the pan.

2   In a large saucepan, combine the butter, coconut oil, nut butter, brown sugar, vanilla, honey, and 2 tablespoons water. Cook over medium heat, stirring frequently, until you have a uniform syrup. Remove from heat. Add the oats, almonds, coconut, chocolate chips, oat bran, sesame seeds, and cinnamon. Stir until the dry ingredients are thoroughly coated. Transfer the mixture to the prepared pan, and press it as firmly into the pan as possible, first using your hands, then using a spatula or wooden spoon to flatten the top. Sprinkle the salt over the top.

3   Bake until the edges darken, 35 to 40 minutes. The mixture will be soft when you take it out of the oven, but allow it to cool completely before taking it out of the pan and cutting into 16 squares.

storage

ROOM TEMPERATURE • covered container, 10 days

FREEZER • cut and stored in a covered freezer-safe container with layers of parchment or waxed paper, 4 months (thaw at room temperature)

POTATO
CHIPS

—or—

the
strangest
thing in
the garden

iT TOOK ME A FEW YEARS of gardening to build up the courage to grow potatoes, and I still can astound my friends with the description of the experience. "I put a chunk of old potato in the ground." (Their eyes grow wide.) "Then it grows into this huge jungle of spindly plants." (No! Really?) "Then at the end of the summer the plants die and the ground is filled with potatoes!" (No way! Are they still out there? Let's go get some!)

The first year I grew potatoes, I ordered far too many seed potatoes from Fedco in Maine, and sitting in my muddy spring garden in April surrounded by carefully cut potato chunks, I couldn't handle throwing any away. Although I had dreams of the kale and tomatoes and beets I would plant that spring, I filled nearly every bed in my garden with seed potatoes. I soon had a jungle of potato plants, and on the vines grew fruit that looked like perpetually unripe cherry tomatoes. Up until this point, I had never actually seen a potato plant, and I was shocked to discover the mysterious fruit.

"Am I supposed to eat that?" I asked a friend as we stood in the midst of my potato forest.

"Only if you want to die a horrible death," she answered.

What a plant! Mysterious and deadly, nurturing and prolific—no wonder whole civilizations have revolved around the life and death of the potato.

We stayed away from the poison green fruit, and as the summer progressed, Joey's enthusiasm about the little tubers in the dirt grew to new levels. Nearly every day he would let me know that he was just going out to "dig a few potatoes," and his nails acquired a constant sliver of dirt beneath them. For a while I tried to tell him to wait until it was really time to harvest, but watching Joey dig with such glee was just too much fun. And so began our love affair with potato chips.

POTATO CHIPS   MAKES 4 TO 6 SERVINGS

1 Preheat the oven to 450°F. Lightly grease two baking sheets with olive oil. Fill a large mixing bowl with water and add ½ teaspoon salt. Stir to dissolve.

2 Using a mandoline, cut the potatoes into $^1/_{16}$-inch slices. (With a knife, you can go a little thicker, and the chips will have a little less crunch.) As you slice the potatoes, submerge them in the salted water and let sit for 5 minutes.

3 Remove the potatoes from the water and press them in a dish towel to dry. Pour the water out of the bowl, dry it, return the potatoes to the bowl, and toss them with the olive oil and the remaining ½ teaspoon salt.

4 Spread the potatoes on the prepared baking sheets in as close to a single layer as you can achieve. Bake the potatoes for 15 minutes, then reduce the heat to 300°F. Rotate the baking sheets and bake for another 15 minutes. Switch the baking sheets and bake again for 15 minutes for a total of 45 minutes. The chips are done when they are golden and dry and start to peel off the baking sheet. Remove the potatoes from the oven to take the chips that are already finished off the sheet. Continue to bake the rest of the chips for another 10 to 15 minutes.

5 When all the chips are ready, spread them on paper towels and sprinkle with salt, if desired.

- 3 tablespoons olive oil, plus additional for the baking sheets
- 1 teaspoon salt, plus additional for sprinkling
- 1½ pounds potatoes (any variety), scrubbed, peels on

storage

ROOM TEMPERATURE • airtight container, 2 weeks (crisp for 5 minutes in a 425°F oven)

FREEZER • freezer-safe container or bag, 4 months (crisped as above)

MIXED ROASTED NUTS

—or—

the everyday made fancy

WHEN THE GIRLS were old enough that we could think of such things, Joey and I set out to rediscover the lost art of the dinner party. In our world, the potluck was the only kind of dinner party there was, and so we went in search of place cards and candlelight and a few new faces across the table.

The only experience that either of us had with a true dinner party was through reading Tolstoy and Austen, so we imagined candlelit tables of civil conversation and bare-shouldered women next to well-dressed gentlemen. With one oven and three feet of kitchen counter, we had to get creative, and we quickly learned that people are just happy to be invited for dinner, and that a few of our own tricks would make the night even more special.

The table is number one: handwritten place cards (sometimes written by children for extra charm), cloth napkins rolled with a bow of twine to conceal stains, a dessert spoon laid above the plate.

We learned to space out a dinner that on any other night we would have eaten all at once. Courses slow down the whole experience, and the luxury of time is one of the real differences between an ordinary dinner and a dinner party.

When it comes to the food, the smallest tweaks make the everyday extraordinary. Quick-pickle carrots for the most gourmet hors d'oeuvre. Whip up some garlic or shallot in a tiny pot of butter (see page 39) next to a loaf of bread and your guests will swoon. And baked in a little of this and a little of that—a bowl of mixed nuts will do the trick every time. Your guests will brush hands as they fight over the hazelnuts, and there you have it—the ice is broken by the time you serve the first course.

Roasted mixed nuts are useful outside of the dinner party setting as well. Once people are invited to dinner, they may start dropping by unannounced, and then you will always have a snack at the ready.

MIXED ROASTED NUTS   MAKES 4 CUPS

1   Preheat the oven to 300°F. Lightly grease a baking sheet.

2   Combine the butter, chili powder, maple syrup, salt, and herbs, if using, in a medium mixing bowl.

3   Add the nuts, tossing until completely coated in the mixture, and spread them in a single layer on the baking sheet.

4   Bake for 15 minutes, then shuffle the nuts around and bake for 15 minutes more before removing from the oven. When the nuts are cool, toss with additional salt to taste.

storage
ROOM TEMPERATURE • covered container, 1 week
FRIDGE • covered container, 1 month
FREEZER • freezer-safe container or bag, 6 months

- Oil (olive oil, canola oil, or butter)
- 2 tablespoons unsalted butter, melted
- 1 teaspoon chili powder
- 1 tablespoon maple syrup
- 1½ teaspoons kosher salt, plus more for sprinkling
- *Optional:* 1 tablespoon chopped fresh rosemary or dill
- 4 cups raw mixed nuts (almonds, pecans, hazelnuts, peanuts, cashews, Brazil nuts, walnuts)

tense moments ~ Anyone who has ever walked away from a tray of roasting nuts for a minute too long knows exactly where the tense moment will be. The key is to roast the nuts just enough to get that perfect crunch, but not so long that they burn. In my oven, with this recipe, that point occurs at about 30 minutes, but you're going to have to watch those nuts for the last few minutes so you can make sure that you catch the magic moment. When you look at the nuts and think they just might be starting to burn, it's time to take them out.

JERKY

–or–

just you and the highway

YOU NEVER KNOW where a flavor will take you.

The jerky section of the pamphlet that had come with my dehydrator had been taunting me, and so I had finally given it a try. I was pulling the dried garlic-flecked meat out of the dehydrator when Joey and the girls got home from school. They tumbled through the door in a hurricane of sneakers flying off feet and backpacks skidding across the floor. Joey walked straight to the counter.

"Ready?" he asked. He's finally learning to ask first before he reaches for a bite off the tray.

With a nod of my head, he popped a piece into his mouth. First there was a smile, then his eyes closed as the flavor propelled him toward the couch.

"Wow. This really takes me back."

"Where to?" Joey's memories seem always to be interwoven with flavor, and I watched to see how this one would play out.

"Between Santa Fe and Denver. That gas station near Raton Pass." With that, his mind drifted away from the kitchen, back to the time when his only responsibility was to keep his car on the road.

Rosie jumped in his lap, as she tends to do, and curled up against his chest. He came back to us slowly and that look in his eye began to fade as he gave her a tight squeeze. I thought about how we don't really give up who we are when we become parents—how so many things we love to do get integrated into our new selves. I watched Joey, halfway between the couch and the highway, and it seemed like just the right place for him to be.

JERKY MAKES 8 OUNCES

1 Lay the meat slices between two layers of paper towel or a clean dish towel. Press on the meat to draw out the moisture, pounding it with your fists or a meat tenderizer.

2 Combine the garlic, maple syrup, soy sauce, salt, pepper, and red pepper flakes in a large mixing bowl, and stir until well mixed. Toss the meat slices in the marinade until thoroughly coated.

3 Lay the meat on a baking sheet in a single layer and refrigerate, uncovered, for 24 hours. This lets the meat absorb the marinade and speeds up the drying process.

4 *If using a dehydrator,* lay the marinated slices in a single layer on greased plastic sheets and dehydrate for 4 hours. *If using the oven,* preheat to 160°F. Lay the meat on parchment-lined baking sheets and bake for 4 hours.

5 Check the meat. It should not be brittle, but should pull away in strings and have no sign of rawness inside. If it is not ready, dehydrate or bake for 1 more hour and check again. Drying times will vary with meat texture and thickness, but most jerkies should be ready in 4 to 7 hours. Cool the jerky entirely before storing.

storage

ROOM TEMPERATURE • covered container, 2 to 3 days

FRIDGE • covered container, 4 weeks

FREEZER • freezer-safe container or bag, 6 months (thaw in refrigerator before eating)

---

tense moments ~ Preparing meat for jerky is not quick and painless. All the fat must be trimmed, as it will go rancid before the meat. Use a sharp knife and embrace your inner *My Side of the Mountain* character. If you are having trouble getting your meat thin enough, first pop it in the freezer for an hour or two to make slicing easier.

- 1 pound lean boneless beef entirely trimmed of fat (how much beef you start out with depends on how much fat you have to trim), sliced ¼ inch or thinner
- 2 tablespoons minced garlic (about 3 cloves)
- 2 tablespoons maple syrup
- 1 teaspoon soy sauce or tamari
- 1 teaspoon kosher salt
- ¼ teaspoon ground pepper
- ¼ teaspoon red pepper flakes
- Oil (if using a dehydrator)

AISLE

3

canned fruits, vegetables, and beans

applesauce

jam

cucumber pickles

sauerkraut

cranberry sauce

put-up tomatoes

roasted tomatoes
for the freezer
canned tomatoes

beans

canning is not scary

CANNING IS NOT SCARY. Like so many other useful skills, canning was once just something that people knew how to do. Families preserved berries and cucumbers in the summer and apples in the fall; they made jam and pickles and applesauce that could sit on the shelf through the winter. It wasn't so much a craft or choice—it was simply necessary. As the food system shifted and the shelves at the supermarket became packed with factory-made jams and pickles and applesauce, home canning was no longer essential to survival and the art lost its place in the yearly routine. Sadly, people became afraid of it.

Food safety is to be taken seriously. But to any warning that you have ever heard or read about canning, I add one footnote: common sense will keep you safe.

Follow the rules. Use clean equipment. Can from established recipes. If your canned food smells funny or there is fur growing in it, don't eat it. If a jar lid doesn't seal, refrigerate it and eat it sooner.

If you have friends to lead you through the process, fabulous. However, if no one is available, and the other person scrutinizing the mason jars at the hardware store didn't get your "it would be so nice to start a canning club!" hints, then allow me to do what I can from a remote location. After a session or two, I promise that you won't need me anymore.

If you have a few quarts of berries, you can whip up a nice batch of jam in an hour or so. After a few batches, canning will just be something that you do. You won't look at the jars on your counter wondering if there is botulism inside, and you'll be able to go through the process without looking at the directions. I love that. And beware— the process can be a bit addictive. Whether it's the miraculous pop of the lids or the sparkling row of hand-labeled goodies, those little jars will wheedle their way into your heart.

before you begin~

START SMALL • Don't try to make more than eight or ten jars at once. The first time I made jam, I made 45 jars of blueberry jam. It was so hot in my kitchen and my girls watched *Mary Poppins,* twice. I thought canning was the circle of hell that Dante forgot. As I learned later, quantity was my mistake.

You need all of the counter space that you can get. So before canning, clear any mess that might be in your kitchen.

the supplies~

You will need

A CANNING SET • These are cheap, and cheaper yet from yard sales, where they tend to be plentiful. A canning set consists of a large pot and a rack for the jars. If your set doesn't come with a *jar lifter,* get one of those, too. You may use it upside down a few times before you figure out why your jars are slipping out of it. A lid lifter, basically a rod with a magnet on the end, is handy for placing lids onto jars without contaminating them with your hands. A pair of metal tongs is also good to have at the ready.

JARS • You can buy them from the hardware store, search through the nooks of the world for antique ones, or order fancy versions online. I typically make jam in pint or half-pint jars, and applesauce and pickles in quart or half-gallon jars, though the size is up to you.

LIDS AND LID BANDS • Although the jars and bands may be reused, the lids, the circular tops for the jars, should be new. The bands are the open circles that screw onto the bottles to secure the lids. You should be able to find a box of lids and lid bands at the hardware store for next to nothing. If you buy jars, they will come with lids and lid bands.

TWO POTS • These are in addition to your canning pot. One pot (which should be big) is to make the jam or pickle brine or applesauce or what have you and the other (which can be small) is to sterilize the lids and bands.

OTHER • A canning funnel is wider than a regular funnel and should be metal, if possible. A ladle will help you out, as will a liquid measuring cup for pouring hot liquids into jars. Some recipes require a plastic knife or chopstick for eliminating air bubbles.

the ingredients~

PRODUCE • Make sure to start out with the freshest possible ingredients. Produce should be clean and unblemished.

PECTIN • For jam, many fruits need some additional pectin to help the gelling process, and I favor Pomona's Pectin. It comes with a handy little piece of paper with recipes, and these are the basis for the jam made by most people I know. Other pectins are available in liquid and gel form, but Pomona's is the only pectin on the market that does not require large amounts of sugar to make it effective as a gelling agent. Pomona's requires additional calcium, a pectin booster, and this comes with the pectin in a separate packet. Follow the directions on the box to make calcium water for the Jam recipe (page 84). High-pectin fruits, such as apples, quinces, and citrus fruits, require no additional pectin.

ACID AND SUGAR • There are two ingredients that prohibit bacterial growth in your canned food: acid and sugar. Jams and jellies have a high sugar content, so as long as you keep that constant, you can create your own recipes. When it comes to canning other foods, it is important to stick to established recipes to ensure the right acid level. A good basic canning book like the *Ball Book of Home Preserving* will give you guidelines for anything that you desire to stuff into a jar.

the canning process

All of the recipes in this book can be processed in a water bath—that is, simply boiled in a deep pot of water. A water bath is a safe method for jam, applesauce, tomatoes (not sauce), and pickles. If you want to take your canning repertoire beyond this list, you will need a pressure canner, which safely cans foods with lower acid levels. A pressure canner enables you to heat the contents of the jars to a higher temperature than a simple water bath, killing bacteria that can grow in low-acid environments. I only cover water-bath canning here, but a pressure canner is a great investment if you want to can everything in your garden or from the farmers' market.

Some recipes, such as Cucumber Pickles (page 86), do not even require a water bath. The heat of the brine is enough to seal the jars, and because they are packed in vinegar, there is a high enough acid level to negate the possibility of bacterial growth. The shelf life for these foods is a little shorter (about 6 months), but you can also process them in a water bath if you would like to extend the shelf life.

1   **COOK** Jams (page 84) are quick to cook, but Applesauce (page 81) takes longer, so make sure that you read through your recipe before you begin. The product should be hot when it goes into the jars, and steps 1 and 2 can happen simultaneously. If the product cools before your jars are ready, reheat before step 3.

2   **STERILIZE** Fill the canning pot three-fourths to the top with water, cover, and set it over high heat until it comes to a boil, about 30 minutes. Immerse the empty jars in the water and boil for 10 minutes. Turn off the heat and leave the jars in the hot water until ready to use. Alternatively, you can sterilize your jars in a hot dishwasher, then leave them on the heated dry setting until ready to use. Wash all necessary utensils in hot, soapy water.

Fill the small pot with water and bring to a boil. Remove from heat, and submerge the lids and bands in the water. Leave them in the water until you are ready to use them, although if the water gets cold, remove the lids and bands, bring the water back to a boil, remove the pot from the heat, and return the lids and bands to the hot water.

3   **FILL** Line up your hot jars on a counter close to the stove. Using your canning funnel and ladle or liquid measure, fill the sterilized jars with the product. Fill to ½ or ¼ inch from the top, depending on your recipe. This space between the contents and the top of the jar is called "headspace," and I specify the needed headspace in each recipe.

4   **POKE** This is necessary for thicker products such as tomatoes, applesauce, or thick jam. Slide a clean plastic knife or chopstick along the inside of the jar to get rid of any trapped air bubbles where bacteria could grow.

5　**TOP** Use a fresh paper towel or clean rag to wipe any excess off the jars. Using clean metal tongs or a jar-top magnet, take each lid out of the water and place it, rubber gasket side down, on each jar. You can touch the top of the lids once they are settled on the jars, but do not touch the bottom or sides of the lids—it is important that they stay sterile. Remove the bands from the water—again, you can touch the outside of the bands but not the inside. Screw the bands on the jars just firmly enough so that they don't feel wobbly on their grooves.

6　**PROCESS** Place the jars into the rack that came with your canning pot, and lower the rack into the hot water. You can probably fit seven or eight jars in your rack. Don't try to fit more jars into the rack than seems comfortable—you can do a second water process with any remaining jars. The water in the pot must be at least 1 inch above the top of the jars, so if there is a long processing time, refill the pot with hot water from a kettle as necessary. Let the water come back to a boil, and from that moment, start timing. Processing time will vary with ingredients, from 10

minutes for most jams to 40 minutes for tomatoes.

7　**COOL** When the time is up, use the jar lifter to remove the jars from the water. Put them on the counter and don't move them. Just perk up your ears and listen. You will probably hear the satisfying sound of some of your jar lids popping right away. Some will take as many as 12 hours. After 12 hours of undisturbed counter time, you can move your jars.

8　**TEST** Check the jar lids for depressed centers (that's what you want). Any jars that have not sealed can be stored in the refrigerator and the contents eaten within the same time as you would any open jar.

9　**STORE** Remove the bands from the sealed jars. Using a wet cloth, wipe off any jam or sauce that has congealed on the outside rim of the jar. This prevents mold from forming on the inside of the band. Store sealed jars on the shelf without bands—save them for when you open a jar and want to store it in the refrigerator. Store in a cool place away from direct sunlight.

a few possible tense moments ~ When I talk to people about what scares them when it comes to canning, the first thing they often mention is breaking glass and exploding jars. I have never had jars break in my canning pot, and I have never exploded a jar. There are, however, a few things that might not go as planned, and all are totally fixable.

THE JAM IS TOO RUNNY If you are using pectin, this probably won't happen. But if it does, can the jam and call it fruit sauce. Your pancakes will thank you.

THE LID DOESN'T POP The most likely culprits for this are too much or too little head space, or you didn't wipe the rim of the jar. Put the jar in the fridge and eat it soon!

SOME LIQUID LEAKED OUT OF THE JARS IN THE WATER BATH, BUT IT SEALS ANYWAY As long as it seals, it is safe to eat. Eat from these jars before the others that did not lose liquid.

THERE IS MOLD GROWING IN THE HEAD SPACE OF MY SEALED JAR I have never had this happen, but it is certainly possible. Don't open the jar—just throw it away.

altitude ~ Because water boils at a lower temperature when you are at a higher altitude, processing times will change depending on where you are. The general rule is to add 5 minutes to your processing time if you are 1,001 to 3,000 feet above sea level, 10 minutes if you are 3,001 to 6,000 feet above sea level, 15 minutes if you are 6,001 to 8,000 feet above sea level, and 20 minutes if you are more than 8,000 feet above sea level.

APPLESAUCE
—or—
our fall

I'M PRETTY SURE IT WAS THE APPLES that turned Joey from a westerner to a New Englander.

Joey grew up in Denver and went to college in Santa Fe. That first fall in New England, we were unemployed, undirected, and newly pregnant. We camped out at my parents' house with countless bowls of cereal and taped episodes of *Buffy the Vampire Slayer*. We spent hours making handwritten invitations for our upcoming wedding while we dreamed up plans for our next step. We took late-summer walks and watched the leaves change, we went apple picking, and we drove to every fall festival within a fifty-mile radius. Each year, we re-create the adventures of that first fall, and not a fall goes by without several trips to the orchard.

Apples might be my favorite fruit to pick. Windy Hill Farm orchard is right down the road, and we pick a bushel in half an hour. Unlike strawberries (sore knees and arms, 100°F in June), the apples seem to jump into our bags and baskets; they hang around our heads and we don't even need to look for the perfect one—it's always within reach. The fruit goes into every lunch and salad and pie, and the rest become lovely pink-hued jars of applesauce.

Applesauce is an endlessly useful substance—dessert, condiment, snack, and baking ingredient. If it's the plain ingredient you need, keep it simple. I'm a cinnamon-maple girl myself, and Sadie eats the stuff for breakfast whenever there is an open jar around. If you want to make a small batch, just scale it back and divide the recipe as your apple supply dictates. Applesauce freezes as well as it cans, so preserve it according to your preference and your freezer or shelf space.

APPLESAUCE MAKES 5 QUARTS

1 Combine the apples and water in your largest pot. Bring to a boil over medium-high heat, then cover and reduce the heat to medium-low. Add the ginger, if using. Cook, stirring occasionally, for 20 minutes, or until the apples start to fall apart.

2 If you are canning your applesauce, start step 2 on page 76.

3 Meanwhile, remove the sauce from heat. Pass the cooked apples through a food mill, with the mixing bowl catching the puree. Return the puree to the pot, and add the lemon juice. If using, also add the cinnamon, maple syrup, or sugar to taste.

4 *To freeze the applesauce,* let cool before transferring to containers. *To can the applesauce,* return the sauce to a low boil and continue with steps 3 through 9 on pages 76–78 (see head space and processing requirements below).

- 16 pounds (30 to 40) apples, cored and quartered, unpeeled
- 6 cups water
- *Optional:* large finger of peeled ginger
- 6 tablespoons fresh lemon juice (from 2 to 3 lemons)
- *Optional:* 1 tablespoon ground cinnamon, maple syrup, or sugar to taste

storage

FRIDGE • covered container, 1 week

FREEZER • freezer-safe containers, 1 year (thaw in refrigerator)

CANNABILITY • head space, $\frac{1}{2}$ inch; processing time, 20 minutes (jars last on the shelf for 1 year)

---

tense moments ~ If you can your applesauce, the sauce will expand a bit more than jam will. Make sure that you allow $\frac{1}{2}$ inch of headspace and keep the sauce hot through the whole process—this will help prevent the applesauce from expanding so much that it leaks out when you remove the jar from the hot water. Also, it is common for the solids to separate from the liquid in applesauce. If there is a bit of liquid at the bottom of your jar, don't worry, just stir the contents of the jar when you open it.

eACH OF THE JARS on my shelf has a story.

I made a batch of black raspberry jam with my friend Meg. She needed a break from her life, and I had just been released from the hospital after an emergency appendectomy, so she temporarily moved into our upstairs room with her two little girls. We were deep into summer, and as soon as I could walk upright, we pushed the limits, threw the girls in the car, and went berry picking. A few hours later we returned home with purple-smeared faces and a huge box of fruit, each berry the size of a thumb.

By 10:00 that night, the kitchen was clean and quiet. Out came the big pot, and the jars sat glowing on the counter. I was tired and achy, but I knew I wouldn't sleep until the jars were filled.

As we picked through the berries, we talked about our day—about her girls and my girls, the strangeness of being thirty, and the pressure to find a passionate occupation. We talked and talked through the bubbling of the jam until it was time to fill the jars with the sweet, purple liquid. Then from that moment until the filled jars were submerged in water, we were silent.

My parents' generation went back to the land to find spiritual awakening and a new community; I go back to the land to feed my family. In my life, I look for ways to act, areas where I can create an effect. And for many of us, we can feel slow change when we turn our kitchens into our own food factories, when we bring our friends together in an assembly line and create a food product we can trust. When we count the jars and line them up, it is not only the jars of jam that make us glow with satisfaction. It is the promise of food put by, of self-sustainability in our kitchens. It may be slow change, but it's real, and it feeds us.

JAM

- 8 cups berries, fresh or frozen (strawberries should be hulled and halved)
- 4 teaspoons calcium water (included in pectin box)
- ¼ cup fresh lemon juice (from 1 to 2 lemons)
- 1½ cups sugar or honey
- 4 teaspoons low-sugar pectin (see page 75)

1   If you are canning your jam, start step 2 on page 76.

2   Meanwhile, combine the berries, calcium water, and lemon juice in a large saucepan. Bring the mixture to a boil and use a potato masher to mash the fruit. Combine the sugar and pectin in a small mixing bowl. Add the pectin mixture and stir vigorously until the pectin is entirely dissolved, 1 to 2 minutes. Remove from the heat. If there is foam on the top of the jam, skim it off with a spoon or a skimmer.

3   *To freeze the jam or store it in the refrigerator,* allow to cool before transferring to containers.

4   *To can the jam,* proceed with steps 3 through 9 on pages 76–78 (see head space and processing requirements below).

storage

FRIDGE • covered container, 3 to 4 weeks

FREEZER • freezer-safe containers, 1 year (thaw in refrigerator)

CANNABILITY • head space, ¼ inch; processing time, 10 minutes (jars last on the shelf for 1 year)

ONE HOT MIDSUMMER MORNING, I had to run to work and leave Joey and the kids carless for the day. They were on summer vacation, and I could tell he was facing the expanse of time with some dread.

"There are cucumbers in the fridge. Make pickles." That was all I had to offer, and I felt a little bad about it as I said it.

Kitchen experimentation is my thing. Joey has a few dishes in his repertoire, and he doesn't venture away from them too often. But there were a lot of cucumbers in the fridge.

When I came home, there they were—lined up in the pantry, ready for their dormant rest time. Not only did Joey make pickles, he filled the jars with edible art: chiles that had been withering in the crisper drawer, bursting dill flowers from the garden, garlic cloves, and nasturtiums.

Now Joey makes grilled cheese, pancakes, omelets, pizza . . . and fantastic pickles.

If you are a first-time canner, pickles are a great recipe to get you started. Because of the high vinegar content, a water bath isn't necessary. The heat of the brine seals the jars, and the acid level of the vinegar is so high that it prohibits bacterial growth. This recipe will last on the shelf for six months, but you can also process in a water bath for ten minutes to extend the shelf life to one year.

CUCUMBER PICKLES   MAKES 10 QUART JARS (5 HALF-GALLON JARS)

- 8 pounds (12 to 15) small cucumbers
- 4½ cups apple cider vinegar
- 4 cups distilled white vinegar
- 10½ cups water
- 1 cup kosher salt
- 6 tablespoons dill seed or flowering tops of 10 dill plants
- *Optional:* dried or fresh chiles, peeled garlic cloves, fennel, peppercorns, mustard seeds, coriander seeds, cloves, nasturtiums, garlic scapes, grape leaves

1   Sterilize your jars, lids, and bands as outlined in step 2 on page 76.

2   Wash the cucumbers thoroughly under cold water. You can keep them whole or slice them into spears.

3   Combine the apple cider and white vinegars, water, and the salt in a large stockpot. Set it over medium-high heat and bring the mixture to a boil.

4   Meanwhile, pack the cucumbers in the jars, dividing the dill and other optional herbs evenly among the jars.

5   Use a ladle to fill the jars with boiling hot brine ½ inch to the top.

6   Top the jars as outlined in step 5 on page 78. Listen for the pop of the lids as they cool. You can leave the bands on the jars in this case—unlike jam, pickles don't make a mess on the outside of the jar, so there is no risk for mold. If a jar doesn't pop, put that jar in the fridge and make it the first jar you open. Store the pickles in a dark place and wait 2 weeks to cure before eating.

storage

FRIDGE • covered container, 2 months

FREEZER • no

CANNABILITY • head space, ½ inch; jars last on the shelf for 6 months, water bath only needed to extend shelf life to 1 year

mAKING FOODS MORE ALIVE in your own kitchen can seem a little bizarre. After all, it is customary to end the life of our food before we eat it.

Hedley and Zoe were friends of a friend, and when Joey and I started throwing dinner parties, they were the first guests on our list. Hedley gave me a big kiss on the cheek and turned her sparkly eyes to the candlelit table with glee. Zoe handed me a handmade paper-cut card and the friendship began.

Hedley has a talent for sourdough, and her care of those magical cultures creates some of the best bread I have ever tasted. Zoe's fermentation skill of choice happens in the ceramic crock—he learned how to make sauerkraut from Sandor Katz, the American fermentation master and author of *Wild Fermentation* (Chelsea Green, 2003). Fermented foods are a perfect antidote to the corn-based diet that has come to feed us over the last several decades; with each bite we increase the diversity of the good bacteria in our bodies.

Fermentation works with conditions in your natural environment to transform foods and beverages, charging them with helpful bacteria that aid in digestion, immunity, and general well-being. Getting the fermentation started is easy—when left at room temperature under only slightly controlled conditions, these super foods just make themselves. Many foods can be enhanced through fermentation; sourdough is made in this way, as are wine, beer, and yogurt. Most vegetables can be fermented with great success, and if you look around at the traditional foods of other cultures there is almost always a fermented pickle in the mix, whether it be preserved lemons, kimchi, or sauerkraut.

You can make your kraut in whatever glass or ceramic vessel that you have available, and the recipe comes together in just a few empowering minutes. In a week or two ordinary cabbage will have transformed into something quite extraordinary.

CANNED FRUITS,
VEGETABLES, AND BEANS

SAUERKRAUT   MAKES ½ GALLON

- 3 pounds cabbage, red or green or a mix of the two, quartered, cored, and thinly sliced
- 1½ heaping tablespoons kosher salt
- *Optional:* ⅓ cup caraway seeds

variation ~ KIMCHI (A SPICY ASIAN SAUERKRAUT)
Add grated carrots, sliced ginger and garlic, scallions, and diced hot peppers.

1 Combine the cabbage, salt, and caraway seeds, if using, in a large mixing bowl. Squeeze the mixture with your hands or beat it with the potato masher or rolling pin. The goal is to break down the cabbage so that it releases its juice—keep working on it until it gets very wet.

2 Scrape the mixture into your ceramic crock or wide-mouthed glass jar, making sure to pour in any liquid that the cabbage has released. Place a small plate over the cabbage and a clean rock or jar to weight down the plate. Press on the weight to draw more brine out of the cabbage. Lay a clean dish towel over the vessel and store in a cool corner of your kitchen. Press down on the weight every few hours to draw more moisture out of the cabbage. Check the sauerkraut after 24 hours. If the brine is not entirely covering the cabbage, add a saltwater solution of 1 teaspoon of salt to 1 cup of water.

3 Keep an eye on your kraut over the coming days to monitor its activity. Some bubbling is a good sign, and a layer of fine white scum is part of the process—just skim it off. Taste the kraut every 3 days or so. You might prefer the taste of the younger kraut and stop there, or you can let it ferment for up to 10 days. If the kraut tastes too salty, let it ferment for 1 more day and try it again. When it is ready, decant it into jars in its liquid and store in the refrigerator.

storage
FRIDGE • covered container, 2 months
FREEZER • no

> **tense moments** ~ My first attempt at sauerkraut didn't go so well—in retrospect, I think that the August heat of my kitchen did in those lovely bacteria. After 10 days of fermentation, I had a salty pot of cabbage mush. If your sauerkraut is mushy or it smells unappetizing, compost it! Next time the process will work, and life is too short to eat bad kraut.

iMAKE CRANBERRY SAUCE from scratch every year. It is always met with wonder.

"You made that, from scratch?"

I try to say "I did!" with my impressive voice, but in the end I have to admit that making cranberry sauce from scratch actually rivals opening a can in ease.

I know there are probably some of you who have an attachment to can-shaped gelatinous "cranberry sauce." Go ahead, eat that. I recognize that holiday food habits are serious and probably shouldn't be broken. Food memories run very deep.

Thanksgiving never fails me. I know some people who dread it; they tell horror stories of canned green beans and alcoholic in-laws and overcooked turkey. Just the thought of that November Thursday brings out the optimist in me, and I can't help but respond to their tales with an invitation to our table for next year. What could be better than a holiday about gratitude, eating, and pie? I can't imagine. When I was a child, we would go around the table and share what we were most grateful for before we dug in. My grandmother would start to cry with the first response, and by the end of the go-around, she'd be fully sobbing into her napkin. She rarely could get her own thankful words out, but her tears made it clear that the list was long.

My grandmother used to make her cranberry sauce with canned pineapple. I could, and did, eat way too much of it in one day, but then I became allergic to pineapple. Since then, I have adapted the recipe to use canned mandarin oranges, and I like that even better. Pineapple or oranges—you decide. Just make it a few days before you intend to eat the sauce, so the flavors can really do their thing.

CRANBERRY SAUCE   MAKES 4 CUPS

1. Combine the cranberries and ⅔ cup water in a medium saucepan. Bring to a boil, cover, and simmer for 15 to 20 minutes, or until the cranberries start to burst. Over this time, stir the mixture occasionally, checking to make sure that there is enough liquid. If the berries are sticking to the bottom of the pot, add ¼ cup more water.

2. After most of the berries have burst, stir the oranges or pineapple and any liquid into the cranberries.

3. Combine the cinnamon, cloves, and cardamom in a small piece of cheesecloth, tie it up, and throw the bundle in the pan. (I like the cheesecloth because it infuses the mixture without adding the elements themselves, but if that feels too fussy, you can add ground spices instead.) Cook, covered, at the lowest heat for 20 to 30 minutes, or until the sauce is thick and all the berries have burst.

4. Remove the cheesecloth packet and stir in the maple syrup. Refrigerate for at least 2 hours before serving.

storage

FRIDGE • covered container, 2 weeks

FREEZER • freezer-safe container, 6 months (thaw in refrigerator)

- 20 ounces fresh or frozen cranberries (organic if possible, as cranberries are heavily sprayed)
- Two 10.75-ounce cans mandarin oranges in juice (or 6 fresh oranges, membranes removed), or one 15-ounce can pineapple chunks (not in syrup)
- 1 cinnamon stick
- 8 whole cloves
- 2 cardamom pods
- ½ to ¾ cup maple syrup

i'M FAIRLY CERTAIN that the secret ingredient in preserved tomatoes is self-forgiveness. I have cried over a counter of moldy tomatoes and I can tell you that it makes the end result far too salty.

If you are searching for a way to preserve the tomatoes on your counter, then you are already in the midst of the whole affair. Perhaps your garden had a burst of activity, or a friend asked you to pick her tomatoes while she was away. I get my tomatoes in fifteen-pound boxes from Indian Line Farm in South Egremont, Massachusetts. The tomatoes are seconds, less than perfect because of their softening skins and alien shapes. When those boxes appear on the shelf, I lose any thought of what I planned to do that night, and I recognize that the time to put up tomatoes is now. Then I get home and there is dinner to be made, and then I have a meeting, and then there is this and that to do, and then . . . there are moldy tomatoes.

You may be a better manager of your time or have endless hours of August ahead of you to devote to peeling tomatoes. But if you are just a bit like me, I offer some wisdom, or at least commiseration.

Tomatoes provide, in their essence, an opportunity to appreciate the moment. All year, there are tasteless imitation tomatoes at the supermarket. In midsummer, we eat the first tomatoes of the season sprinkled with salt and pepper, shoved into the mouth with juice running down our arms. They are precious, and every fruit is devoured. By the end of the summer, tomatoes are so plentiful, it is hard to imagine a time without them. If only all of those tomatoes could be saved—think of how delicious they will be in January! So I scramble to preserve them, but in the end, the first freeze gets that last of them and it is time to embrace the fall.

ROASTED TOMATOES FOR THE FREEZER

MAKES 7 TO 9 CUPS

- 6 pounds ripe tomatoes, cored and halved
- 1 head of garlic, cloves separated and peeled
- Fresh herbs (oregano, thyme, basil)
- Salt and pepper
- Olive oil

ALTHOUGH I OFTEN HAVE OTHER ASPIRATIONS for my tomatoes, most of them end up roasted in freezer bags. These are easy to make and store, and what you have in January is a bag full of ready-made sauce. Sauté an onion, and throw a thawed bag of roasted tomatoes on top of it over medium-low heat for 20 to 30 minutes.

1 Preheat the oven to 275°F. Line two jelly-roll pans with parchment paper.

2 Lay the tomatoes on the tray, cut side up. Scatter the garlic cloves over the tomatoes, then scatter the herbs. Give both trays a shake of salt and pepper and a drizzle of oil.

3 Roast for 5 hours. Remove and let cool. Pour the contents of the trays, including the olive oil and juices, into freezer bags.

storage

FRIDGE • covered container, 3 days

FREEZER • in freezer bags, 4 to 6 months (thaw in refrigerator)

CANNED TOMATOES   MAKES 7 QUARTS

CANNING TOMATOES IS MESSY. Wear an apron, clear your counters, and give yourself over to the process. At the end of the day you will have a shelf filled with lovely red jars.

- 20 pounds ripe tomatoes (45 to 60)
- 14 tablespoons bottled lemon juice (more predictable acid level than fresh)

1 Start step 2 on page 76.

2 Fill a medium saucepan with water and bring to a boil over high heat.

3 Fill a large bowl with ice water. Using a paring knife, cut a small *x* in the bottom of each tomato. Submerge the tomatoes a few at a time in the boiling water for 30 seconds, then transfer to the ice water. The tomatoes will slide right out of their skins.

4 Fill a teakettle with water and bring to a boil. Place the sterilized jars on the counter, taking care not to touch the rim or inside of each jar.

5 Lift each peeled tomato out of the ice water and remove the core with the paring knife. (You can remove the seeds from the tomato if you'd like.) Then stuff the tomatoes into the jars. You should be able to get about 7 tomatoes into a quart jar.

6 When the jars are full, poke as outlined in step 4 on page 76 to remove air bubbles.

7 Pour 2 tablespoons of lemon juice into each jar, then pour the boiling water from the teakettle over the tomatoes, filling the jar to ½ inch from the top.

8 Proceed with steps 5 through 9 as outlined on page 78 (see head space and processing requirements below).

storage

FRIDGE • open jar, 1 week

CANNABILITY • head space, ½ inch; processing time, 45 minutes (jars last on the shelf for 1 year)

BEANS
—or—
feeding the world

IT HAS ONLY BEEN THROUGH my infrequent brushes with spirituality that I have come to know the magic of beans.

My mother was something of a seeker in the eighties, and we spent our fair share of time dressed in orange and were gifted with new names like Chandra and Rupi. As a kid, just the word *meditation* would bring on a roll of my eyes, but as a teenager, when I heard tales of the Vipassana meditation center in Shelburne Falls, Massachusetts, my ears perked up. No gurus, no processing of childhood woes, no religious denominations—it would just be me and a cushion and a room full of people trying to pay attention to their own breath. I was sixteen and I felt I could survive anything, but ten days of silence and no dinner nearly ended me. After the final day, however, I miraculously felt ready to finish the rest of my year of high school, and I couldn't wait to return to the meditation center.

My next visit took me straight into the kitchen. As fulfilling as I had found my first retreat, this time there was a new education in store for me, and feeding the center's students was more of a revelation than sitting in that hall myself. I was assigned to a small team in the kitchen, and together we cooked the porridge for breakfast, the simple vegetarian lunch, and set out fruit for the evening snack. I learned how little food it takes to feed a whole room of hungry people, and that with a good-sized bag of beans, everyone will walk away happy and full.

Beans prepared at home create a velvety broth that simply cannot be re-created with beans from a can. Many thanks to my friend Julie Scott for converting me to the oven method— the slow heat cooks them gently, preventing breakage and increasing the creaminess of the broth. Frozen beans maintain far more flavor, nutrition, and digestibility than their store-canned counterpart. To re-create the convenience of a can of beans, get out your Dutch oven, cook those beans, and freeze them.

BEANS   MAKES 6 TO 8 CUPS COOKED BEANS

1 Preheat the oven to 250°F.

2 Rinse the beans and put them in a large, oven-safe pot (a cast-iron Dutch oven is ideal). Cover the beans with water to within 4 inches from the top of the pot. You want at least three times as much water as there are beans.

3 Set the pot over high heat and bring to a boil.

4 Cover, move the pot to the oven, and cook for 3 to 6 hours, or overnight, checking after a few hours to monitor their progress, if possible. Don't cook longer than 8 hours—otherwise the beans will break down and will be more of a soup.

- 1 pound dried beans (black beans, cannellini, pinto, kidney—any except lentils, split peas, or adzuki)

storage

FRIDGE • covered container, 3 days

FREEZER • cool beans and pour with their liquid into freezer-safe containers, leaving 2 inches for expansion, 6 months (to use, thaw in the refrigerator or microwave)

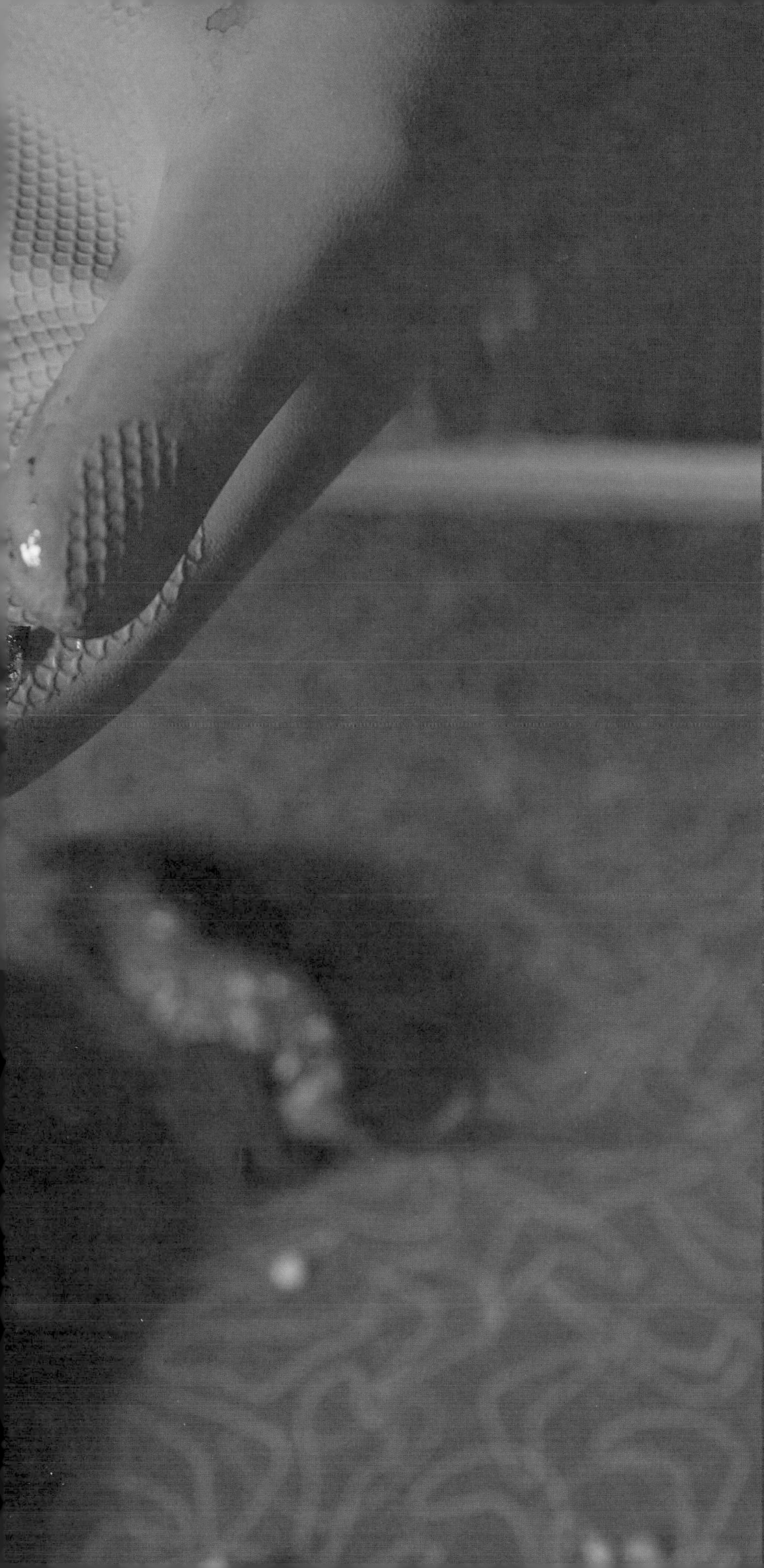

AISLE

4

condiments, spices, and spreads

ketchup

mustard

salsa

hot sauce

salad dressing

italian dressing

buttermilk ranch
dressing

mayonnaise

hummus

nut butter

spice mixes

poultry spice

curry powder

5-spice powder

J

JOEY AND I fell in love at Blake's Lotaburger in Santa Fe. Since then, we've had a thing for unexpected hamburgers. We search them out, critique them, and drive long distances for them. That night at Blake's was the first time Joey held my hands over a plastic table while our names were shouted over the loudspeaker, but it was certainly not the last.

Joey has a food talent of his own, and I am not the only one who gets emergency food calls. If you are looking for that really good diner you heard about years ago, you're calling Joey. He's passionate about his road food, and I am passionate about my homemade food, and some people assume that this is a difference between us. It's just not true. I have had to win him over when it comes to homemade food, but I was actually a road-food lover before I ever set eyes on Joey.

There is a roadside burger stand in New Milford, Connecticut, with barely a sign to mark it. You never know when it will be open, but Clamp's is worth the drive. Joey found it at the end of a cross-country odyssey, and after taking a bite of his perfect burger with caramelized onions, he resolved to get me there. A year later, we stole an August afternoon and headed over the state line, and as I sunk into bliss with my burger, I snuck a peek at him sitting on the other side of that plastic table. He was just watching me.

"Every time I eat a really good burger, I think about you."

Dates like this make marriage feel possible.

This search for the ideal burger is a quest that Joey and I are on together. Sometimes Joey takes me to places like Clamp's. Other nights I bake buns in our kitchen—we make patties from local beef, and we chop up a few of Joey's pickles. Then . . . I make condiments.

This ketchup uses every spice on your rack, but it's worth it. Adjust the spice to your own liking and make a big batch to can or freeze. If you're searching for that perfect burger, with the right condiments, it might be on your own table.

KETCHUP MAKES 4 CUPS

- 2 tablespoons olive oil
- 1 cup diced onion (1 large)
- 5 garlic cloves, minced
- 6 pounds ripe tomatoes, peeled, seeded, and cored, or three 28-ounce cans tomatoes, drained
- 3 teaspoons kosher salt, plus additional to taste
- 1 tablespoon paprika
- 1 teaspoon ground cinnamon
- ¼ teaspoon ground cloves
- 1 tablespoon celery salt
- ½ teaspoon ground cumin
- ¼ teaspoon dry mustard
- 1½ tablespoons chili powder, plus additional to taste
- ½ teaspoon ground pepper
- ¼ cup apple cider vinegar
- ¼ cup distilled white vinegar
- 1 tablespoon packed light brown sugar, homemade (page 51) or store-bought
- 1 tablespoon honey

1 Heat the olive oil in a large, heavy-bottomed pot over medium heat. Add the onion and cook until translucent, about 3 minutes. Add the garlic, and cook for 1 minute, while stirring.

2 Add the tomatoes, salt, paprika, cinnamon, cloves, celery salt, cumin, dry mustard, chili powder, and ground pepper and simmer, covered, stirring occasionally, for 20 minutes.

3 Blend until smooth with an immersion blender or transfer the mixture to an upright blender in two batches and puree until smooth. If transferred, return the mixture to the pot.

4 If you are canning the ketchup, start with step 2 on page 76.

5 Add the vinegars, brown sugar, and honey. Cook over medium heat, uncovered, stirring often, until the ketchup thickens, about 30 minutes. Adjust salt, pepper, and chili powder to taste.

6 *To freeze the ketchup,* let cool before transferring to containers. *To can the ketchup,* continue with steps 3 through 9 on pages 76–78 (see head space and processing requirements below).

storage

FRIDGE • covered container, 2 weeks

FREEZER • freezer-safe container, 6 months (thaw in refrigerator and whisk to re-emulsify)

CANNABILITY • head space, ½ inch; processing time, 30 minutes (jars last on the shelf for 1 year)

i EAT EXACTLY TWO BRATWURST A YEAR, and I eat them seven days apart. It might just be my favorite week—bookended by the last weekend in September and the first in October—it's fall festival time in the Berkshires.

We begin with the Apple Squeeze, an event that takes over the entire town of Lenox, Massachusetts. The stores spill out onto the sidewalks with marked-down summer clothes and crafters fill tables with crocheted scarves and hand-forged wind chimes. Before the cider donuts and the fried dough, we insist on protein, and so we keep our eyes peeled for the faux trolley-car cart that has the best bratwurst anywhere.

The next weekend is the Harvest Festival, a fundraiser for our local botanical garden and my favorite of the two festivals. We buy tickets for the girls for the haunted house, the straw-bale maze, and the pony ride. We give them each a dollar for the book tent so they can pick out four books. While we wait for the girls to make their choices, we listen to mediocre folk music and eat our second bratwurst of the week sold by the same faux trolley cart, this time with a side of sweet potato chips cut with a drill and deep-fried at the stand next door.

We don't know where those bratwurst come from. We don't know where that cart lives all year, or who makes those football-shaped rolls that hold up to kraut and mustard with minimal sog. But there is always mustard on my shirt by the end of those festivals, and I wear it as a badge to show the world that I know how to eat a bratwurst well. Wherever you find your perfect bratwurst (or hot dog, or whatever your fancy!), make sure you bless it with the very best toppings. Use just the right amount of sauerkraut and don't skimp on the mustard.

MUSTARD MAKES 1½ CUPS

- ½ cup brown or yellow mustard seeds
- ⅓ cup red wine vinegar
- 2 garlic cloves, minced
- 2 teaspoons salt
- 3 tablespoons honey

1   Pour the mustard seeds into a medium mixing bowl and cover with water 3 inches higher than the seeds. Cover the bowl, and let it sit at room temperature for 12 hours.

2   Drain any remaining water from the seeds. Combine the soaked mustard seeds, the vinegar, garlic, salt, honey, and ¼ cup water in a blender, and blend until smooth. Transfer the mixture to a jar, cover, and refrigerate. The mustard will be spicy for the first few days, but will mellow over time.

storage
FRIDGE • covered container, 2 months
FREEZER • no

O KAY, LET'S HAVE IT OUT.

I hate cilantro.

I'm one of those people who think cilantro tastes like soap, and I'd happily eat your soap if you gave me a choice between the two. People ask me if it's an allergy, and sometimes I say yes. Does it count as an allergy if being in the same room with it makes me want to scream and clench my face? Does it count that when I eat it accidentally, the taste tortures me for days?

I've heard that there is a cilantro-hating gene, and I've also heard that in cultures where children eat cilantro from a young age, there are no cilantro haters. My friend Lauren, an Italian-American cilantro hater, told me that Northern Italy has more cilantro haters than any other place, but I don't have an ounce of Northern Italian blood in my body.

People ask me how I live without salsa, and of course I can't live without salsa! Luckily salsa, like most things, is better when it's made at home. There is no cilantro in my recipe—then it just wouldn't be mine—but by all means feel free to add it to yours.

SALSA MAKES 4 CUPS

- 2 pounds (4 to 5 medium) ripe tomatoes, cored and quartered
- About 1 small red onion, roughly chopped
- 2 garlic cloves, roughly chopped
- 1 red bell pepper, stemmed, seeded, and roughly chopped
- 1 or 2 hot chile peppers, stemmed and seeded
- ½ cup loosely packed parsley, roughly chopped
- 1 sprig fresh oregano, leaves roughly chopped
- 4 tablespoons fresh lime juice (from 2 to 3 limes)
- 2 teaspoons salt, or more to taste

1 Set the tomatoes in a fine-meshed sieve and allow them to drain for 5 minutes.

2 Combine the tomatoes, onion, garlic, red pepper, and hot peppers to taste in the food processor. Pulse with the chopping blade two or three times, or until the ingredients are just combined. Add the parsley, oregano, lime juice, and 2 teaspoons of salt, and pulse one more time. Adjust the salt to taste.

storage

FRIDGE • covered container, 5 days

FREEZER • fresh salsa, no (roasted variation in a freezer-safe container for up to 4 months)

CANNABILITY • no

---

tense moments ~ The texture of your salsa will vary based on the water content of your tomatoes. If you end up with salsa that is too liquidy to sit on a chip, you have two options:
1. Call it gazpacho! Now you have a first course for your dinner, and it's fancier than salsa.
2. Set the salsa over a strainer lined with cheesecloth to remove some of the liquid. I prefer this method so I can use the spicy tomato juice for Bloody Marys to drink with my chips and salsa.

variations ~

- **ROASTED SALSA** Substitute half or all of the tomatoes with husked and halved tomatillos. Roast the tomatoes, tomatillos, red onion, red pepper, and hot pepper in a 400°F oven for 45 minutes. Let cool, then combine in the food processor with lime juice, parsley, oregano, and salt.

- **CHUNKY SALSA** Don't use the food processor; chop the ingredients to your desired size and combine.

S TANDING OVER A KITCHEN COUNTER as we cook, kitchen fears often make it into the conversation.

"Raw eggs!"

"Botulism!"

"What if I feed my guests something terrible at a dinner party and I just have to watch everybody eat it?"

There are as many different kitchen fears as there are people who cook. But it is so worth it to push on, to take warnings from the cooks in your family, magazines, or any other source in stride and keep your wits about you—except in the case of truly frightening items in your kitchen. Like hot chiles.

Living in New Mexico instilled in me a deep respect for the hot chile, and I always took pride in my ability to tolerate the burn. I read instructions to don rubber gloves with scorn, claiming that I wanted no barrier between myself and the chile. I went through periods of five-minute blindness after I rubbed my eye in the midst of chile preparation, sneaking bits of coconut oil and other home remedies from the pantry to try to mellow the burn.

One day, I started experimenting with hot sauce. I'd been collecting a glorious rainbow of random chiles from the farmers' market and farm share. I had roasted them in the oven, set to work peeling them, and pulsed them in the Cuisinart. Then I opened the lid.

The physical burst from the air in that food processor knocked me back. I was unable to breathe for a moment, and then I knew I was facing a really fantastic hot sauce. I stuck my finger into the red puree, and confirmed it—it was the best hot sauce I had ever had. By dinnertime, my hands were bright red, and I showed Joey the blisters. He had no sympathy. "Maybe now you'll wear gloves like everyone else."

And now I do. So make hot sauce—but open the window, and please wear rubber gloves.

HOT SAUCE MAKES 1½ CUPS

- 1 pound mixed hot chiles
- 1 cup distilled white vinegar
- 1 tablespoon salt
- 1 tablespoon lime juice (from ½ lime)
- 2 tablespoons honey

1 Preheat your broiler (on a medium setting, if it has one), and set a rack 10 inches from the top of the oven. Line a baking sheet with aluminum foil or parchment.

2 Lay the chiles on the sheet and puncture each with a fork. Broil until the chiles are black and bubbling, 5 to 10 minutes depending on the heat of your broiler. Flip the chiles with tongs and broil until the other side is black and bubbly.

3 Remove the baking sheet from the oven and put all the chiles in a medium bowl. Cover the bowl with plastic wrap. Let sit for 15 minutes, then the chiles will be ready to come right out of their skins.

4 Put on your gloves. Slide each chile out of its skin, then remove the stem and as many seeds as you can.

5 Transfer the chiles into a food processor or blender and add the vinegar, salt, lime juice, and honey. Blend until smooth, about 1 minute.

storage

FRIDGE • covered container, 6 weeks

FREEZER • freezer-safe container, 6 months (thaw in refrigerator)

CANNABILITY • no

M Y FIRST RESTAURANT JOB was at a place that inspired frenzy in all who dined there. Its specialty was Japanese food— the food was decent and the sushi was fresh, if a bit overpriced. What brought people back with that crazed look in their eye, however, was the green salad dressing.

That was the first of many restaurants that I worked in, and fantastic salad dressing was a link between them all. Other restaurants didn't have the magical green dressing, but each had its own signature mix—a vinaigrette or creamy concoction that had people finishing endless salads just so that they could mop up the dressing that remained.

Salad dressing is easy. The secret is to be creative.

Here are two classic salad dressings—Italian and Buttermilk Ranch. With a whisk and a little imagination, nothing can stop you from making your very own magical dressings.

ITALIAN DRESSING   MAKES 1½ CUPS

- ¾ cup olive oil
- ¼ cup white wine vinegar
- ¼ cup fresh lemon juice (from 1 to 2 lemons)
- 4 tablespoons chopped fresh parsley, or 4 teaspoons dried
- 4 garlic cloves, finely minced
- 2 tablespoons chopped fresh basil, or 2 teaspoons dried
- 1 teaspoon red pepper flakes
- 1 teaspoon dried oregano
- 1 teaspoon salt
- Black pepper, to taste

1   Combine all the ingredients in a 2-cup jar and screw the lid on tightly.

2   Shake for 10 seconds. If you are using dried herbs, let the dressing sit for 15 minutes to rehydrate the herbs. Adjust the black pepper to taste.

storage
FRIDGE • covered container, 2 weeks (shake to re-emulsify before serving)

FREEZER • no

BUTTERMILK RANCH DRESSING   MAKES 1½ CUPS

- ½ cup Buttermilk, homemade (page 41) or store-bought
- ½ cup Mayonnaise, homemade (page 117) or store-bought
- ¼ cup plain Yogurt, homemade (page 30) or store-bought
- Squeeze of fresh lemon juice, to taste
- 1 teaspoon minced fresh parsley
- 1 tablespoon minced fresh chives
- Salt and pepper to taste

1   Combine all the ingredients in a small bowl or 2-cup jar with wide mouth.

2   Whisk until smooth. Adjust the salt, pepper, and lemon to taste.

storage
FRIDGE • covered container, 4 days
FREEZER • no

MAYONNAISE
—or—
unplugged

n O MATTER HOW MUCH you love the yellow label and plastic jar (and I do!), you will love the homemade version even better.

Because I am a girl who loves her gadgets, I always stubbornly try to make mayonnaise in my food processor. That never works (the yolks slide elusively under the blade), and then another friend teaches me again with a whisk. I'll tell you with conviction—mayonnaise requires a whisk and a steady hand, no more.

I was in Istanbul when this finally sunk in. My friend Molly was living there with her husband, Aurel. I had just celebrated my thirtieth birthday, and my friend Lissa her fiftieth, and we decided that it was a good excuse for a life-changing Turkish adventure. Our ten days in Turkey also coincided with Aurel's birthday, and on that morning, he had asked for only one treat for his celebration: deviled eggs. Lissa set about gathering ingredients. Aurel is French, so when a recipe calls for mayonnaise, he reaches for the eggs and olive oil. As I gathered our supplies for a picnic, I heard a musical tinkling coming from the kitchen. I snuck into the room.

There were Lissa and Aurel. He was whisking bright yolks as she poured fragrant, green olive oil into the bowl. They were so focused, I held my breath so as not to disturb them. In seconds, the mixture had turned thick and yellow. He stuck a finger in, gave it a taste, and exhaled with a wide and joyful grin. *"Oui."*

There is a satisfaction in the creation of mayonnaise that can be matched by few other foods. I still hold up the bowl with pride as Joey chops carrots for the next day's lunches. He's unimpressed—the alchemy of this has never excited him, but then he oohs and ahhs over his sandwich.

MAYONNAISE MAKES 1 CUP

1 Whisk together the egg yolk and 1 teaspoon of water in a medium mixing bowl.

2 Using a measuring cup with a spout, pour a few drops of the olive oil into the egg yolk and whisk vigorously. Then add a few more drops and whisk again. Continue this until you have a thick yellow sauce, then add greater amounts of oil at once.

3 Add a squeeze of lemon and a pinch of salt, and whisk again. Whisk in the mustard, if using. Adjust the lemon and salt to suit your taste.

- 1 large egg yolk (this won't be cooked, so good and local, if possible)
- 1 cup olive oil
- Fresh lemon juice, to taste
- Salt, to taste
- *Optional:* 1 teaspoon Dijon mustard

storage

FRIDGE • covered container, 4 days

FREEZER • no

---

tense moments ~ There is a moment when your mayonnaise could separate or break—the result is a watery mixture of egg and oil. The culprit is most likely over-hasty pouring of the oil at the beginning of the process. You really want to just do a few drops at a time to start. Don't worry—it's still savable. Crack a new egg yolk into a clean bowl, and very slowly pour the broken sauce into the yolk while whisking, just as you did the first time with the olive oil. Stay patient while you pour, and it will work for you the second time.

HUMMUS

—or—
the gift

WHEN I DESTROYED THE MOTOR of yet another blender while making hummus, it was time to get a food processor. We didn't have the money for such gadgetry at the time, and so I placed an ad in our local paper: "Grateful cook seeks free Cuisinart."

My phone rang the day the ad came out. The woman on the phone lived nearby, and I hurried over right away. The Victorian house was sunken into the hill like the setting for a Hitchcock film, and the front door led right into the kitchen. The room was a work of art—gadgets and tools dating back to the fifties and all surfaces used to their greatest advantage: copper pots hanging from makeshift racks on the ceiling, and shelves lining every wall filled with spices, canned goods, and condiments. Cookies were in mid-process and it was snowing flour, and the tiny ageless woman shuffled ahead of me, making her way through the whole scene. She claimed that she had lived there for thirty years—how had I never met this woman or seen her on the street? Her kitchen entranced me, and I secretly hoped that she would invite me for tea.

In a moment, it was over. She burrowed into a cabinet, emerged with an ancient food processor, and plopped it into my arms.

"Thank you very much," she said, and shooed me out of the kitchen. She was already walking away from me, and by the time I got my thanks out, she had disappeared.

I cooked a pot of chickpeas that night, and in the morning I filled the freezer with silky hummus. I never saw my kitchen angel again, but with every pulse and whir I thanked her. Years later, I took the spent food processor to the dump with a special reverence, and although I was finally able to replace it with a shiny new one, I still think about it.

This is my friend Audrey Sussman's famous hummus recipe that sells out at our farmers' market every week. It makes a big batch and freezes beautifully.

HUMMUS MAKES 7 CUPS

Combine the chickpeas, garlic, lemon juice, tahini, salt, cumin, cayenne, parsley, and olive oil in the food processor. Blend until smooth and uniform. If the hummus is too thick, add 1 to 2 tablespoons cooking water or can liquid from the chickpeas and blend again. Taste, and add additional garlic and salt if needed.

storage

FRIDGE • covered container, 4 days

FREEZER • freezer-safe container, 6 months (thaw in the refrigerator)

- 7 cups cooked chickpeas, either store-bought canned or from 1 pound dried chickpeas (reserve cooking liquid or can liquid to use later in the recipe)

- 10 to 15 garlic cloves, roughly chopped

- ⅔ cup fresh lemon juice (from about 3 lemons)

- ½ cup tahini (sesame paste)

- 1½ teaspoons kosher salt, or more to taste

- 1 teaspoon ground cumin

- ¼ teaspoon cayenne

- ½ cup packed chopped fresh parsley

- 2 tablespoons olive oil

NUT BUTTER

—or—
nearly
perfect

nUT BUTTER IS A PERFECT FOOD, especially when you make it at home.

It's inexpensive, delicious, and an all-purpose form of protein that can be spread on anything for extra punch. Rule #4 of good parenting: when in doubt, spread it with nut butter.

Homemade nut butter has a number of advantages over store-bought. You have control over all of the elements, so sweetness, saltiness, and texture is up to you. Roasting the nuts just before blending them brings the most wonderful flavor to the butter, and there is no pesky oil separation to deal with, like when you open a jar of store-bought nut butter. It also needs to be used up within a month, so having some of your own nut butter around is an excellent excuse to make peanut butter cookies.

Of course, there is that one issue that can't be solved. Homemade or store-bought, there is no cure for peanut butter fingers (which turn into peanut butter couch, peanut butter backseat, and peanut butter everywhere). Especially when a toddler is at the table, it's all a parent can do to spring out of her chair and tackle the kid posthaste, before the peanut butter fingers coat the whole house.

So nut butter is nearly perfect, which is good enough for me. But if you find the cure for peanut butter fingers, let me know. This method can be used for peanuts, almonds, or any other nut.

NUT BUTTER MAKES 1½ CUPS

1 Preheat the oven to 350°F. Spread the nuts on a baking sheet and roast for 10 to 15 minutes, or just until they begin to brown. Remove the baking sheet from the oven and allow the nuts to cool slightly.

2 Place the nuts, salt, and honey in the bowl of a food processor fit with the chopping blade. Blend for 20 seconds. With the motor still running, drizzle 3 tablespoons of oil into the bowl through the chute in the lid, and process for 30 seconds. If the nut butter is still dry, continue to blend and add the additional tablespoon of oil. Process for up to another minute to reach your desired consistency. Taste and adjust for salt, if needed.

- 1 pound (3½ cups) shelled raw nuts
- ½ teaspoon kosher salt, plus more to taste
- 2 teaspoons honey
- 3 to 4 tablespoons canola or peanut oil

storage
ROOM TEMPERATURE • no
FRIDGE • covered container, 1 month
FREEZER • no

tHE FIRST TIME I SAW REAL SPICES was in the grand bazaar in Marrakesh, where I visited briefly during a stint as a personal assistant. I had an hour to wander one of the largest open-air markets in the world. I could envision an entirely new kitchen at home waiting to be created: exotic jars of smoked cardamom pods and aromatic cumin seeds, garlands of cloves and dried chiles.

I have, at times in my life, not lived up to my potential, and this was one of those instances. I can feel myself in Marrakesh again, the perfume of vanilla and cumin and dates, the battering calls of money in many languages. I can see myself overwhelmed by the array before me, arms crossed, unable to let any of it in. I left the bazaar with three small yellow bags of curry powder. I gave them away as gifts when I got home, and I promised I would do better if I had the chance again.

A year and a half later, I was on my own time, walking through the arched pathways of the spice bazaar in Istanbul with my friend Lissa. We spent all day there, comparing apricots, learning the difference between cheap and real saffron, and sampling Turkish delight. I left with bags full of aromatic and inspiring ingredients. They were like little manifestations of the changes that had happened in my life in the past year. I had decided to leave my job, to try to make a living by connecting to people with food. The smell of cinnamon sticks and star anise clung to everything, and I felt like I could be inhaling at any time in history.

It can be hard to see the power of a good spice when we are so used to bottles of flakes and powders at the store, but any spice blend can be re-created and made better. Look at what goes into the mix; if it's a seed mix, like curry powder, buy the spices whole. If it's an herb mix, like poultry spice, buy the elements individually and mix them to your liking. The mix will be far fresher and more flavorful, and you'll never want to go back to the old bottles.

CONDIMENTS, SPICES, AND SPREADS

POULTRY SPICE   MAKES 4 TABLESPOONS

- 4 teaspoons dried thyme
- 4 teaspoons dried marjoram
- 1½ teaspoons dried rosemary
- 1 teaspoon ground black pepper
- 1½ teaspoons dried sage

Combine the thyme, marjoram, rosemary, pepper, and sage in a jar and cover with the lid. Shake to combine.

storage
ROOM TEMPERATURE • airtight jar, 3 months
FREEZER • airtight jar, or doubled freezer bags, 1 year

CURRY POWDER   MAKES 6 TO 8 TABLESPOONS

- 10 cardamom pods
- 1 tablespoon coriander seeds
- 1 cinnamon stick, broken up
- 1½ teaspoons cumin seeds
- 1 teaspoon yellow mustard seeds
- 1 to 2 dried hot chiles, to taste
- 2 tablespoons ground turmeric

1   Combine the cardamom pods, coriander seeds, cinnamon stick, cumin seeds, mustard seeds, and chiles in a small skillet. Toast over medium heat, shifting the pan around to keep the spices moving. When the seeds start to pop and they become more aromatic, 2 to 4 minutes, remove from the skillet.

2   Break open the cardamom pods to release the seeds inside. This can be done in a mortar and pestle or by putting the pod on a cutting board and pressing it with a spoon.

3   Put the toasted spices, cardamom seeds, and ground turmeric in a coffee grinder reserved for spices or mortar and pestle. Grind the spices together until they make a fine powder. Let cool, and transfer to a jar.

storage
ROOM TEMPERATURE • airtight jar, 3 months
FREEZER • airtight jar, or doubled freezer bags, 1 year

5-SPICE POWDER MAKES 4 TABLESPOONS

1   Combine the peppercorns, cloves, cinnamon stick, fennel seeds, and star anise in a small skillet. Toast over medium heat, shifting the pan around to keep the spices moving. When the seeds start to pop and they become more aromatic, 2 to 4 minutes, remove from the skillet.

2   Put the toasted spices in a coffee grinder reserved for spices or mortar and pestle and grind them together until they make a fine powder. Let cool, and transfer to a jar.

- 1 tablespoon black peppercorns
- ½ teaspoon whole cloves
- 1 cinnamon stick
- 1 tablespoon fennel seeds
- 6 star anise

storage
ROOM TEMPERATURE · airtight jar, 3 months
FREEZER · airtight jar, or doubled freezer bags, 1 year

---

dry your own herbs ~ A few pots in a windowsill can produce enough herbs to get you through the winter, or you can collect fresh herbs from the farmers' market in the summer to dry at home. To dry, most herbs do well in a warm and shady spot laid out on a wire screen for 10 days. Herbs with a higher moisture content, such as mint and basil, do better in a dehydrator. Either way, lay them out to dry while still on the stem; then remove from the stem and store in an airtight jar or double-bagged in the freezer.

i WAS A VEGETARIAN for most of my childhood. It came to an end when my aunt put a steak in front of me at the Clement Street Grill in San Francisco with the claim that I would wither away without some good meat on my plate. I was seventeen, and I've been a meat-eater ever since.

Because the majority of meat production and processing is more disrespectful to life and more dangerous than we could ever imagine, I stopped buying most of the meat for our family at the grocery store. We are lucky that in our area there are many dedicated farmers raising animals on grass, giving them a good life and a humane death. I am also fortunate to have a big chest freezer. It is in my basement, and I share it with my vegetarian farmer friends, Jen and Pete, who fill their half with frozen corn and spinach.

You can buy meat piece by piece at farmers' markets, sometimes from a farm stand freezer at a farm, and occasionally at a good gourmet food store or butcher. You can also purchase an entire animal, or at least part of one. This is almost like hiring the farmer to raise an animal you have purchased, and it is usually more cost-effective than buying meat piece by piece. This is how I purchase most of my meat, and because I worked hard to acquire it and paid good money (well spent!), there's no way I'm throwing away the bones.

A well-made broth will heal your soul and stay in your memory. A boxed or canned broth will do neither, and my recipe is somewhere in between. Every time we eat meat, I save the bones in a big bag in the freezer. When I have an afternoon and a spare onion, I pack the bones into my soup pot with a few vegetables and let them simmer away. I store the stock in my freezer, and then I have a good base for soups and stews.

Here is a guideline for stock, but feel free to improvise. An onion is fairly essential, but beyond that, use what you have. Many thanks to Nigel Slater for teaching me that an added tomato imparts a golden hue and deep flavor to stock.

STOCK   VARIES WITH THE QUANTITY OF BONES

- Chicken, pork, or beef bones (fresh or frozen)
- 1 large onion, cut in half
- 2 carrots, cut into 3-inch chunks
- 4 garlic cloves
- 2 celery ribs, cut into 3-inch chunks
- 1 leek (white and green parts), cut into 3-inch chunks
- 1 ripe tomato
- 1 dried bay leaf
- A few sprigs of fresh thyme, or 1 teaspoon dried
- A few sprigs of fresh parsley, or 1 teaspoon dried
- 10 whole black peppercorns
- Salt, to taste

1   Pack the bones, onion, carrots, garlic, celery, leek, and tomato into a soup pot. Tuck the bay leaf, thyme, parsley, and peppercorns into the mix. Fill the pot with enough water so that it is 1 to 2 inches over the contents of the pot. Bring to a boil and skim off any foam.

2   Reduce the heat to low, and cook, covered, for at least 2 hours, but up to 4 hours, or until the stock has a good, rich flavor.

3   Set a sieve over a mixing bowl and pour the stock through the sieve. Taste and add salt as needed or salt when you use it. Let the stock cool in the refrigerator and skim off the fat if you wish.

storage
FRIDGE • covered container, 3 days
FREEZER • freezer-safe container, 6 months (thaw in refrigerator or microwave)

variation ~ The method for vegetable stock is very similar. Use fresh vegetables—you may be tempted to use the withered leeks in the back of your fridge, but you will get a withered and tired vegetable stock. Combine any vegetables that you have, keeping in mind that leeks, onions, carrots, garlic, and celery are always winners. Broccoli stems and kale stems are good here, as is celery root, and of course, a tomato. Add herbs and peppercorns as in the meat stock and cook, covered, over low heat for 1 to 2 hours. Strain.

W HEN I WAS A CHILD, there was only one cookbook in my mother's kitchen that mattered.

I remember sitting on the floor of our
communal house in the hippy outskirts of Boston as I perused
the handwritten recipes of "mushroom strudel," "cauliflower
cheese pie," and "heavenly compotes." I liked the hand-drawn
pictures and the "apple-honey custard pie" the best. I was
pretty sure that my mother had written the book, and it made
me love it even more.

I looked at the smile in the author photo, and I was cheered
by the thought of my mother and her daffodils, standing in a
magical place called Ithaca. The book was written in her handwriting, and the letters were so familiar to me from shopping
lists on the fridge, handwritten song lyrics scattered around
the house, and inspirational "breathe" notes in the bathroom.

The book was published a year before my birth, so my
mother must have been busy then—crafting recipes and creating whimsical illustrations of zucchinis and tostadas. She
would have been twenty-two by the time the book was com-
pleted and I was starting to grow in her belly. The cover of the
book was perfect and simple, the title arched above a few simple vegetables. It was called *Moosewood Cookbook*. Underneath
were the words "By Mollie Katzen."

I figured my mother had a secret identity. She was, after all,
queen of the tofu meatball and knew everything there was to
know about tamari. And her lentil soup recipe? Perfect.

Those handwritten words, spoken in a voice of Mollie and
Mom combined, taught me how to cook.

Sadie once picked up my copy of the *Moosewood Cookbook*
and asked, "Did you write this? This is your handwriting!"

My mother still makes the best lentil soup, and I am thankful to Mollie Katzen so I can carry on the tradition. I've
changed it a bit to my taste and offer my version here, so that
Sadie can have it in her mama's very own words.

LENTIL SOUP   SERVES 6 TO 8

- 2 tablespoons unsalted butter
- 1 cup chopped white onion
- 1 teaspoon salt, plus more to taste
- 1 tablespoon minced garlic
- 1 cup minced celery
- 1 cup chopped carrots
- 3 cups raw green lentils or French lentils, rinsed
- 1 dried bay leaf
- 1½ cups peeled and chopped potatoes
- 7 to 9 cups Stock, homemade (page 130) or store-bought, or water, or some combination of the two
- Black pepper, to taste
- 2 tablespoons fresh lemon juice (from 1 lemon)
- 1½ tablespoons packed light brown sugar, homemade (page 51) or store-bought
- 1 teaspoon tamari or soy sauce
- *Optional:* 2 tablespoons red wine; fresh oregano, fresh parsley, or fresh thyme, for garnish

1   Heat the butter in a large soup pot over medium heat until melted. Add the onion and sauté until shiny, about 2 minutes. Add the salt, garlic, celery, and carrots to the pot and cook over medium heat for 5 minutes, or until aromatic and shimmering.

2   Add the lentils, bay leaf, potatoes, and 7 cups of the stock or water to the pot. Bring to a boil, then reduce the heat to medium-low and simmer covered, stirring occasionally, for 2 hours, or until the soup is creamy and the vegetables are soft. Check the consistency of the soup over that time—if it is too thick or seems dry, add the additional water or stock.

3   Thirty minutes before you serve the soup, add the pepper, lemon juice, brown sugar, tamari, and wine, if using. Remove the bay leaf. Taste and adjust the salt as necessary. Serve the soup with fresh oregano, parsley, or thyme, if you'd like.

storage

FRIDGE • covered container, 4 days

FREEZER • freezer-safe container, 6 months (thaw in refrigerator or microwave)

WHEN SADIE WAS YOUNG, I embarked on that journey of homemade baby food that so many others have traveled before me. I had a brick of a book instructing me how to use ice cube trays in ways that I had never imagined, and I carried a mini food mill in my bag. I was in control and ready for success.

Unfortunately, Sadie and I were no good at this one. There were always congealed purees in my hair and on my clothes, and I grew to despise my mini food mill. Still, I persevered, terrified that I might screw up my child with less than perfect nourishment. I cranked everything through the mill, and Sadie spit it all out at me.

When Rosie popped her first tooth, the scene was very different. I had the comfort of knowing that I had not harmed my first child with some horrible parenting mistake, along with the chaos of two children under age two. She, too, hated the orange and green purees, and so when two-year-old Sadie insisted on feeding her sister whatever she was eating, I waved my hand in acceptance.

A few years later a delayed love for pureed vegetables kicked in. It was a rough winter, and we all seemed to need the simplicity of a bowl of smooth and creamy soup at least twice a week. The girls each developed a favorite that they still ask for regularly—potato leek for Sadie and roasted butternut squash for Rosie. When I have a surplus of ingredients, I whip up a quick batch of puree and freeze it in family dinner–size containers. A day ahead of time, the container goes in the fridge to thaw, and then making dinner is as easy as adding a bit of milk or cream to the puree and cutting a loaf of bread to dip in the soup. Sure, I've failed in the task of feeding my kids perfect and nutritious food on more occasions than I can count. But I hope a good bowl of soup emptied into a little belly on a regular basis will make up for it.

ROASTED BUTTERNUT SQUASH SOUP

MAKES 4 QUARTS (SERVES 10 TO 12)

- 1 tablespoon olive oil
- 7 pounds (2 to 3) butternut squash
- 1 head of garlic, cloves separated and peeled
- 10 sage leaves
- 5 to 7 cups Stock, homemade (page 130) or store-bought, or water
- Salt and pepper
- 1 cup whole milk
- *Optional:* Crème Fraîche, homemade (page 28) or store-bought; roasted squash seeds (see Note); 2 slices bacon, chopped

note ~ Rinse the seeds with water, remove any squash membrane, and dry the seeds thoroughly. Toss with a tablespoon of olive oil and 1 teaspoon salt, and bake on a parchment-lined tray for 15 minutes in a 275°F oven.

1 Preheat the oven to 400°F. Grease two large baking dishes or jelly-roll pans with olive oil.

2 Cut each squash in half lengthwise by setting it upright on your counter and cutting straight down. Scoop out the seeds with a spoon and compost or set aside for roasting (see Note). Lay each cut squash face down on your dish, and lift it up to tuck a few garlic cloves and sage leaves into the cavity. Place in baking dishes. Roast the squash for 60 to 90 minutes, or until the skin starts to bubble and the "meat" is very soft. The timing of this will entirely depend on the size of your squash.

3 When the squash are ready, remove them from the oven, turn them over to release the steam, and let cool for at least 30 minutes. Using a small knife or spoon, separate the squash pulp from the skin and throw the pulp and the garlic in a soup pot. You can either add the sage leaves to the pot as well, or set them aside to use to garnish the finished soup.

4 Add 5 cups of the stock and blend thoroughly, either with an immersion blender in the pot itself or by blending in batches in a upright blender. If the soup is too thick, add the additional stock, ½ cup at a time. Add salt and pepper to taste. If you are freezing the soup, do so now, before adding the milk.

5 To serve the soup immediately, add the milk, then more salt and pepper to taste if needed. Reheat, if necessary. Serve as is, or garnish with crème fraîche, roasted squash seeds, or chopped bacon fried with leftover sage leaves.

storage

FRIDGE • covered container, 3 days

FREEZER • puree (without the milk), 6 months (thaw in refrigerator or microwave, reheat with milk, salt, and pepper, and blend if necessary for a smooth texture)

POTATO LEEK SOUP   MAKES 2 TO 3 QUARTS (SERVES 8 TO 10)

- 1 tablespoon unsalted butter
- 2 tablespoons olive oil
- 2 large leeks, cleaned and chopped, using all of the whites and the lower half of the green
- 2 pounds potatoes, peeled or unpeeled to taste, and quartered
- 5 to 7 cups Stock, homemade (page 130) or store-bought, or water
- ¾ cup whole milk
- Salt and pepper, to taste

1   Melt the butter and olive oil in a medium soup pot over medium heat. Add the leeks and sauté until soft and shiny, about 5 minutes.

2   Add the potatoes and 5 cups of the stock. Cover, bring to a boil, and then reduce the heat to a simmer. Cook, covered, stirring occasionally for 20 to 30 minutes, or until the potatoes fall apart when poked with a fork.

3   Using an immersion blender, blend in pot until smooth; otherwise transfer to an upright blender and puree in batches. Blend for only a few seconds at a time—potatoes can transform to a glue texture with too much blending. If the soup is quite thick, add the additional stock, ½ cup at a time. If freezing the soup, do so now, before adding the milk.

4   To serve immediately, return the soup to the pot and add the milk, salt, and pepper. Reheat, if necessary.

storage

FRIDGE • covered container, 3 days

FREEZER • puree (without the milk), 6 months (thaw in refrigerator or microwave, reheat with milk, salt, and pepper, and blend if necessary for a smooth texture)

BEEF STEW

—or—

what you make

I WORK AT THE FARMERS' MARKET most Saturday mornings through the summer and fall. On one particular October day, the temperature hovered around 35°F, and another woman and I shivered and chatted in our shady back corner of the market, holding warm cups of coffee to bring feeling back into our hands.

We talked about nubby roots and vibrant frost-sweetened greens, and she asked me what she should do with celeriac.

"Well," I began, trying not to let my voice get high and excited as it does when I answer these sorts of questions. "Any kind of soup or stew. Or roast it up. But if you really want to make it shine, it has to be beef stew."

"Oh," she sighed wistfully. "I just don't make beef stew."

Now, this woman works full time, and she balances her career and her family with great skill. If she is at work too late in the day to make a pot of beef stew, I forgive her entirely. In fact, I'll bring her some of mine. But this got me thinking.

For most people, there are things that we make and things that we don't. Usually this has something to do with what our parents cooked for us when we were young, but sometimes it's more random—a friend gave you a recipe for baked mac and cheese in college, you made it, and now you're someone who makes baked mac and cheese.

So I am determined to turn you into a beef stew maker. Here's a basic recipe, but you can change it, and don't let a missing element stop you. If you have exciting vegetables, by all means add them to the mix. Celeriac (celery root), a gnarled, brown, celery-flavored root that shows up in the fall, is my favorite; and kohlrabi, that green or purple vegetable that can only be described as UFO-like, will take your stew up a notch. Anything rooty and starchy will be perfect, and you can serve the stew over noodles, rice, couscous, polenta, or nothing at all.

BEEF STEW

SERVES 6 TO 8 (CAN BE DOUBLED OR TRIPLED)

- 2 pounds cubed beef stew meat, chuck or shanks
- ½ cup all-purpose flour
- 3 tablespoons paprika
- 1 teaspoon salt, plus more to taste
- Freshly ground pepper
- 2 tablespoons olive oil, plus more if needed
- 2 celery ribs, in 1-inch pieces
- ½ pound carrots, peeled and cut into 1-inch pieces
- 1 large onion, sliced lengthwise into 1-inch boats
- 4 garlic cloves, minced
- 1 leek, in 1-inch pieces (all the white and half the green)
- *Optional:* 1 tablespoon tomato paste
- 1 pound potatoes, peeled and quartered
- ½ bottle red wine; or 1 bottle dark beer; or 2 cups Stock, homemade (page 130) or store-bought
- 2 dried bay leaves
- 2 sprigs fresh parsley, or 1 teaspoon dried
- 2 sprigs fresh thyme, or 1 teaspoon dried
- Additional stock or water as needed
- *Optional:* 1 dried chile, a few cloves, chopped green chiles

1 Preheat the oven to 275°F. Wash the meat in a colander and dry thoroughly with paper towels. Really dry it— Julia Child made the hard-won discovery that meat must be entirely dry in order to brown it correctly, and we must honor her legacy by doing the right thing!

2 In a medium mixing bowl, combine the flour, paprika, 1 teaspoon salt, and 5 grinds of pepper or ½ teaspoon pepper.

3 Heat 1 tablespoon of the oil in a Dutch oven or large roasting pan with lid over medium heat. As the oil heats, toss the meat, a few pieces at a time, in the flour mixture. When the oil starts to shimmer in the pan, lay as many pieces of the meat in the pan as you can fit so they don't touch. Cook for 2 to 3 minutes on each side, or until browned but not burnt. Remove the browned meat from the pan, set it aside on a plate, add ½ tablespoon of oil to the pan, and repeat with remaining beef.

4 When all of the beef is browned, add the remaining ½ tablespoon of oil to the pan. Throw in the celery, carrots, onions, garlic, and leek, and shuffle them around with a spatula or wooden spoon until the onions are translucent and the celery, carrots, and garlic have browned a bit, about 5 minutes. Stir in the tomato paste, if using. Add the potatoes.

5 Pour the wine, beer, or stock into the pan and bring to a gentle boil, using your spatula or wooden spoon to scrape up browned bits on the bottom of the pan. (These bits are the base for most of the flavor in your sauce, so don't skip this step!) Transfer the beef to the pot, and add enough stock or water so the entire mixture is almost covered in liquid. Bring back to a boil. Tuck the bay leaves, parsley, and thyme into the liquid. Add the chile, cloves, or green chiles, if using.

6 Cover the pot and transfer to the oven. How long you cook your beef stew in the oven is up to your schedule. It can be ready to eat in 2 hours, but it will be more fantastic after 4 hours, and after 6 hours the meat will dissolve into the sauce and it will become a transcendent thing. However you do it, taste and add additional salt and pepper, if needed. Remove the bay leaves and herb stems before serving.

storage

FRIDGE · covered container, 3 days (best on the second day)

FREEZER · freezer-safe container, 6 months (thaw in the refrigerator or microwave)

---

composting ~ With all of the new composting techniques out there, even the smallest city apartment can have a compost pile. Composting diminishes the amount of trash that you create in your kitchen and creates a great fertilizer for your garden. You can build or buy a fancy container, or you can just start a little pile in your yard where the pile will break down and enrich the soil around it. The general rule of thumb is to keep your pile limited to vegetable and grain material, leaving meats and fats out of it. For compost to be used in your garden, add a dry material like dead leaves or straw.

If you don't have a garden or even a window box that would benefit from your finished compost, offer it to a friend who does. And even if your compost never reaches a garden, the fact that you have created less garbage for the landfill makes the process very worthwhile in itself.

PANCAKES AND WAFFLES

—or—
the division of labor

aFTER NEARLY A DECADE OF MARRIAGE, there are certain things I do not do. I do not mow the lawn, use an electric drill, grill, or make pancakes.

The fact that I have delegated these tasks to Joey continues to pull on me. Every time he walks away from a skillet full of bubbly pancakes expecting me to know when to flip them, I cringe at the sound of my "How big are these bubbles supposed to be?" Sizzling pancakes, when left in my incapable hands, will rarely puff to the height that his do and will often burn.

Joey is not necessarily a natural driller, griller, or pancake flipper. He has some unique skills, however: he will make a mix tape so good you'll keep it forever; he'll always create a hand-made paper-cut mobile for your birthday card; and he can play Mozart by hitting his fingertips against his teeth. But he is the son of a poet, and his father taught him that the manly arts in life are not about hammers and grill tools, they are about love.

When Joey and I were just married, we divvied up the tasks and roles, and our understanding of what husbands and wives do certainly contributed to how we took on our assignments. Childbearing and breastfeeding, of course, fell to me, and so at first, Joey was the breadwinner. Bills and money organization? All me. Ikea furniture assemblage? Always Joey. Dinner? Me. Breakfast, Joey.

At first we weren't really so good at any of it. But then we practiced, and the jobs became skills that only one of us had.

As life changes, we shift into new roles to cover all that needs to be done. I know I will have my turn at each job in time, and the truth is that Joey's not so skilled with that drill, after all. There is a flip side—a warm comfort in knowing that certain bases are always covered. Joey will always make a birthday card better than anything I could find. I have the only lawn with a heart mowed into it to entertain low-flying planes. And I don't need to know how to make the perfect pancake—there's already a plate of them waiting for me in the kitchen.

READY MIX   MAKES 8½ CUPS

Combine all the ingredients in a large jar or container. Whisk until thoroughly combined.

storage

ROOM TEMPERATURE • covered container or bag, 3 months (with whole wheat flour, 1 month)

FRIDGE • covered container or bag, 4 to 5 months (with whole wheat flour, 3 months)

FREEZER • freezer-safe container or bag, 6 to 8 months (use directly from the freezer)

- 8 cups (2 pounds, 8 ounces) all-purpose flour, or substitute 4 cups with whole wheat flour
- ¼ cup sugar
- 2 tablespoons baking powder
- 1 tablespoon baking soda
- 1 teaspoon salt

WAFFLES   MAKES 4 CUPS OF BATTER, ENOUGH FOR 8 MEDIUM WAFFLES

1 Preheat the oven to 200°F. Beat the egg whites to soft peaks with a mixer fit with the wire whip. Set aside.

2 In a small bowl or large liquid measure, whisk together the egg yolks, melted butter, buttermilk, milk, and vanilla.

3 Scoop 2 cups of mix into a medium bowl. Stir the wet mixture into the dry mix until combined, then stir in a big spoonful of the beaten egg white. Using a silicone spatula, gently fold the remaining egg whites into the batter.

4 Grease your waffle iron and scoop ½ cup of batter into the hot iron. Cook per the machine's instructions, use tongs to remove the waffles from the iron, and keep the waffles in a 200°F oven until serving.

- 2 large eggs, separated
- 4 tablespoons (½ stick) unsalted butter, melted and slightly cooled
- ¾ cup Buttermilk, homemade (page 41) or store-bought
- 1 cup whole milk
- 1 teaspoon Vanilla Extract, homemade (page 165) or store-bought
- 2 cups Ready Mix (see above)
- Cooking spray or oil for the waffle iron

storage

FRIDGE • batter, covered container, 3 days; waffles, covered container, 2 days (reheat in the oven or toaster)

FREEZER • batter, no; waffles, wrapped in plastic and in freezer bag, 4 months (reheat in the oven, microwave, or toaster)

PANCAKES MAKES 4 CUPS OF BATTER, ENOUGH FOR TWENTY-FOUR 3-INCH PANCAKES

- 2 large eggs

- 2 tablespoons unsalted butter, melted and slightly cooled, plus additional (or bacon fat) for the pan

- 1 cup Buttermilk, homemade (page 41) or store-bought

- 1 cup whole milk

- 1 teaspoon Vanilla Extract, homemade (page 165) or store-bought

- 2 cups Ready Mix (page 143)

1 Whisk together the eggs, melted butter, buttermilk, milk, and vanilla in a large liquid measuring cup.

2 Scoop 2 cups of the mix into a medium mixing bowl and gently stir the wet mixture into the dry mix. Stir until the mixture is uniform, but there can be a few lumps. Let the batter sit at room temperature for 15 minutes.

3 Heat a skillet or griddle over medium heat, and melt the butter or bacon fat in the skillet. Using a ¼-cup measure, scoop out as many pancakes into the pan as you can fit without them touching. Continue to cook until bubbles pop up on the surface of each pancake, about 2 minutes. Flip the pancakes with a spatula, and cook for another minute or so. (If reserving cooked pancakes, let cool before wrapping for the fridge or freezer.) Repeat with the remaining batter, adding a touch of additional butter or bacon fat to the skillet when needed.

storage

FRIDGE • batter, covered container, 3 days; pancakes, covered container, 2 days (reheat in a skillet or warm oven)

FREEZER • batter, no; pancakes, wrapped in plastic and in freezer bag, 4 months (reheat in a skillet, oven, or microwave)

I HAVE ALWAYS BEEN MORE CAREFUL than I want to be, and I hope that life will be long so that I can continue to practice my "danger" skills. Sadie has inherited the careful gene from me, whereas Rosie careens through the world at breakneck speed. Here I am doing that thing that parents do—putting one child into one box and the other child into another.

The girls continue to show me the folly of this box making.

One winter day, Sadie and I took a hike after school. It was cold, and snowy and rainy, and surprisingly lovely all around us. I took baby steps down the snow-covered path and Sadie laughed at me and let go of my hand. Sadie, my careful child who struggles with her bike for fear of tipping, who didn't jump until she was four years old, galloped down the icy mountain, a tiny superhero with her hair flying behind her like a cape. She skidded to a stop every few seconds to look up at me.

"Come on, Mom!"

When she finally did fall, sliding butt-first into the slushy ground, she looked surprised and then burst into laughter.

"I never imagined that I would fall!"

We both made it down the mountain without a scratch. I took Sadie's ice-cold hand in mine and we headed for the car. I had had enough risk for the day, and when we got home, I made cornbread.

Cornbread, just out of the oven with butter, is safety in a pan. You can make cornbread in half an hour and it will be good as long as it stays warm. There are plenty of foods for brave days. There are caramels and soufflés and delicate cuts of meat. But some days it just has to be cornbread. This slightly sweet cornbread is inspired by a recipe from *The King Arthur Flour Baker's Companion* (Countryman Press, 2003). It is entirely risk-free, quick to make, and will never fail you.

CORNBREAD   SERVES 6

- 4 tablespoons (½ stick) unsalted butter, melted, plus additional for greasing the pan
- 1 cup (5 ounces) all-purpose flour
- 1 cup (4.75 ounces) yellow cornmeal
- 1 tablespoon baking powder
- 1 teaspoon salt
- 2 large eggs
- 1 cup Buttermilk, homemade (page 41) or store-bought
- ¼ cup maple syrup

1   Preheat the oven to 425°F. Lightly grease an 8-inch square or 9-inch round baking pan with butter.

2   In a medium mixing bowl, combine the flour, cornmeal, baking powder, and salt and whisk together until thoroughly combined.

3   Break the eggs into a large measuring cup and beat them with the whisk. Add the buttermilk, maple syrup, and melted butter to the eggs and whisk together until uniform.

4   Add the wet mixture to the dry ingredients and stir to combine with just a few strokes. Pour the batter into the prepared pan and bake for 20 to 25 minutes, or until the cornbread is lightly browned, pulling away from the sides of the pan, and a cake tester or butter knife comes out clean when inserted into the center.

storage

ROOM TEMPERATURE • covered container, 1 day

FRIDGE • no

FREEZER • freezer bag, 3 months (only for cornbread stuffing)

mY MOTHER is barely over five feet tall, has bright eyes, wild hair, and a fair amount of spunk. As soon as I could stand at the stove, she taught me how to steam broccoli to the right crunch, how to create a dinner from anything in the refrigerator, and most important, how to sing while I cook.

My mother does not bake, and although she has put up with my love affair with the oven even when she was sure that the stovetop was the only essential tool we needed, I went one step too far when I ventured into the realm of pie crust. In our two-person family, Orenoke's frozen pie crust was the height of deliciousness. I still relish a frozen crust now and then—when that tinny crunch hits my mouth, I am in the most comfortable moment of childhood, singing '80s pop with my mother at the kitchen counter. I roll my crusts anyway. I have found a quiet spirituality in the marriage of butter and flour that thrills me, and the taste (although a far cousin from frozen pie crust) is, I would argue, better.

When I first took on the challenge of making pie crust, the butter and flour evaded me. Recipes never seemed to call for enough liquid, and so I would add more, and my pastry dough would turn to goop. When Sadie lost a tooth on the crust of my strawberry rhubarb and Rosie ate all the filling out of a perfectly shaped pie-angle, I almost lost hope.

In her book *Bakewise* (Scribner, 2008), Shirley Corriher shared the recipe that changed it all for me. She offered many ways to make that perfect pie crust, but one stood out to me: put it in the stand mixer.

I've only made good pie since, and now I'm getting a bit of a reputation for it. I've tweaked and shifted Ms. Corriher's recipe to suit my own kitchen, but the method remains the same. My mom still says she's not a baker, but I have a rolling pin over here with her name on it, and with the right song on the stereo, I know it'll happen.

BASIC PIE CRUST   MAKES TWO 9-INCH PIE CRUSTS

- 1 cup (2 sticks) cold, unsalted butter, plus additional for greasing the dish
- 2¼ cups (11.25 ounces) all-purpose flour, plus additional to flour the counter and the dish
- 2 teaspoons apple cider vinegar
- ½ teaspoon salt

storage

FRIDGE • in disc or rolled out in pie dish, wrapped in plastic or waxed paper, 3 days

FREEZER • in disc or rolled out in pie dish, wrapped in plastic or waxed paper and in freezer bag, 6 months (thaw in refrigerator before rolling disc, frozen crust in dish can go straight to oven, provided it is not in a glass or ceramic pie dish)

1 Cut the butter into ½-inch squares and combine with the flour in the bowl of a stand mixer. Using your hands, toss the mixture to coat the butter in the flour. Put the bowl in the freezer. In a measuring cup, combine ⅓ cup water, the vinegar, and salt. Stir until the salt dissolves and put the measuring cup in the freezer. Freeze both mixtures for 10 minutes.

2 Take the mixing bowl out of the freezer and blend the mixture on low speed with the paddle attachment until it starts to become the texture of crumbly meal. Take the measuring cup out of the freezer and, with the mixer still running on low speed, slowly pour the wet mix into the bowl. The dough will be crumbly at first, then after 10 or 20 seconds, it will come together in a ball. Stop the mixer.

3 Turn the dough out onto the counter and press it together into a large disc. Cut the dough in two equal parts, wrap each piece in waxed paper, and press each into a disc. Refrigerate for at least 1 hour, and up to 3 days.

4 Grease a 9-inch pie dish with butter and give it a light dusting of flour. Take the dough out of the refrigerator 15 minutes before you are ready to roll it out. Unwrap the dough and place one of the discs on a lightly floured counter. Starting from the center, use your rolling pin to shape the dough into a circle about 12 to 14 inches in diameter and ¼ inch thick.

5 Fold the crust in half, then fold that semicircle in half again so that you have a quarter of a circle. Line up the corner of the quarter with the center of your pie dish and unfold the quarter into a semicircle, then into the full circle.

6 Fill the crust with your pie filling. Repeat the rolling process with the second disc of dough, and either lay it on top of the filling, or cut in strips to form a lattice. Use your fingers to crimp the edge of the dough along the circumference of the pie dish.

GRAHAM CRACKER CRUST

MAKES TWO 9-INCH PIE CRUSTS

- 3½ cups graham cracker crumbs, from 15 to 20 Graham Crackers, homemade (page 220) or store-bought, smashed with a rolling pin in a sealed bag or chopped in a food processor

- ¾ cup (1½ sticks) unsalted butter, melted

1 Combine the graham cracker crumbs and melted butter in a medium mixing bowl with your hands until the crumbs are thoroughly saturated with butter. Press the mixture into two 9-inch pie dishes with your hands. Then use a measuring cup to press it down even firmer into the corners and sides.

2 Refrigerate for 30 minutes. Fill the crusts, or if your recipe calls for a pre-baked crust, bake for 15 minutes in a 375°F oven and cool before filling.

storage

FRIDGE • mixture or pressed in crust, wrapped in plastic or waxed paper, 3 days

FREEZER • unbaked or baked crust, in pie pan, wrapped in plastic and in freezer bag for 6 months (can go straight from freezer to oven, provided it is not in a glass or ceramic pie dish)

variation ~ For a chocolate cookie crust, replace the graham crackers with the chocolate cookie from The Sandwich Cookie (page 276).

O N DAYS WHEN I CANNOT FOLLOW RULE #1 of sane parenting (never take more than one child to the supermarket at a time!), my girls and I inevitably spend 20 minutes in that zone between buckets of carnations and the "freshly baked muffins!" studying the Dora sheet cakes, the upright Disney princesses with their chiffon cake gowns, and the Thomas roll cakes. The miserable teenager in the fake chef's hat ignores us as the girls press their noses against the glass case. They can almost taste that hard blue frosting, and in their minds it is ambrosia. Birthdays are far off, but they try on these cakes for size, imagining their own names scripted in lovely red #5 gel.

When the time comes to actually plan the birthday party, they never ask for those perfect cakes. Rosie begins her cake decision six months in advance, climbing into bed with me first thing in the morning on a nearly daily basis saying, "For my birthday . . ." Both girls create some challenge for me, a flavor combination that I've never done before. I'd buy one of them a Dora cake if they asked for it—a birthday is a birthday and I have nothing to prove. But year after year, I make layer cakes— leaning cakes with funny writing and letters left off of their names where I ran out of space. They forgive me for my lack of perfection and skill with the pastry bag, for the swirled blobs of frosting that I call roses, proudly reporting to their guests that their mom got this cake to look pink by using beet juice.

Birthday-cake making isn't for everyone, so do what inspires you and what you have time for. But if you're looking for a recipe, this is it. As for frosting roses, you're on your own.

This is adapted from the 1-2-3-4 cake that Alice Waters (*Fanny at Chez Panisse*, HarperCollins, 1997) brought into my kitchen. When Sadie developed an egg sensitivity, I created an egg and sugar-free version as well. Top your cake with Whipped Cream (page 279), fresh fruit, or Best Frosting (page 157).

YELLOW CAKE

- 1 cup (2 sticks) unsalted butter, at room temperature, plus additional for greasing
- 3 cups (12 ounces) sifted cake flour, more for dusting
- 4 teaspoons baking powder
- ½ teaspoon salt
- 4 large eggs, separated
- 1½ cups sugar
- 2 teaspoons Vanilla Extract, homemade (page 165) or store-bought
- 1 cup whole milk

storage

ROOM TEMPERATURE • unfrosted cake, wrapped in plastic, 2 days

FREEZER • unfrosted cake, wrapped in plastic then freezer bags, 3 months (thaw at room temperature)

variation ~ For an egg- and sugar-free cake, sift together 3 cups cake flour, 3 teaspoons baking powder, 1 teaspoon baking soda, and ½ teaspoon salt. Combine 1 cup whole milk, ⅔ cup canola oil, 1 cup maple syrup, and 2 teaspoons apple cider vinegar in a measuring cup. Beat 1 cup of butter until fluffy, then add the vanilla. Add the flour mixture and the milk mixture alternately to the batter, starting and ending with the flour. Transfer to your pans and bake as directed in the master recipe.

1   Preheat the oven to 350°F. Cut parchment paper to the size of the bottoms of two 9-inch round cake pans, three 8-inch round cake pans, or two 12-cup muffin tins. (If you are making cupcakes, line the cups with paper liners or just grease them with butter.) Grease the parchment paper with butter and dust the insides of the pans with flour. Tap off the excess.

2   Combine the flour, baking powder, and salt in a medium mixing bowl.

3   Pour the egg whites into the bowl of a stand mixer. Beat with the wire whip attachment until the whites hold soft peaks. Gently transfer to another bowl and rinse out the bowl.

4   Put the butter in the mixer bowl. With the paddle attachment, beat the butter until it's light and fluffy, about 1 minute. Add the sugar, and continue to cream for 1 more minute, until fluffier. Add in the egg yolks one at a time, beating after each addition. Add the vanilla and beat again.

5   When the mixture is uniform, alternately add a third of the flour and a third of the milk and repeat until the full quantities have been used. Mix on a low speed, just incorporating each addition before you move on to the next step. Stir a third of the egg whites into the batter with a wooden spoon; then gently fold in the rest of the whites with a silicone spatula.

6   Pour the batter into the prepared pans, creating a bit of a divot in the center to counter doming in the finished cakes. (If you are making cupcakes, fill the cups only three-quarters to the top.) Bake until a cake tester or toothpick comes out clean, the cakes are golden, and the batter is coming away from the sides of the pan. This takes 35 to 40 minutes for a cake and about 25 minutes for cupcakes, but watch for doneness. Let cool for 5 minutes in the pan, then gently invert and let the cakes cool on a cooling rack. Cool entirely before frosting.

i

F YOU ARE GOING TO GO to all that trouble to make your very own cake, let's just go all the way with it. Set your butter and your cream cheese on the counter, and while it warms we'll talk about frosting.

I aspire to a frosting that is as good as the cake itself, a frosting that does not get left in large globs on the plate. When it comes to a simple frosting, too much powdered sugar is the villain that creates a frosting that does not get finished, so I use a cream cheese base for tang and seriousness. There are all sorts of frostings that we could talk about here—exciting projects that involve a candy thermometer and quite a bit of egg separation—but you may have guests walking in the door and you need frosting now, or at least as soon as they go through those party snacks on the table. We'll make a frosting that everyone loves and that is worthy of the beautiful cake you have created.

BEST FROSTING

MAKES 3¼ CUPS; ENOUGH TO COVER AND FILL A 9-INCH DOUBLE LAYER CAKE, AN 8-INCH TRIPLE LAYER CAKE, OR 24 CUPCAKES

1 Combine the cream cheese and butter in the bowl of a stand mixer and beat with the wire whip until well combined. Add the powdered sugar in ¼ cup increments, tasting after each addition.

2 When you have reached your desired sweetness, add the salt and vanilla and continue beating until your frosting is thick and smooth.

storage

FRIDGE • covered container, 1 week

FREEZER • freezer-safe container, 6 months

- 1 pound cream cheese, at room temperature
- ¾ cup (1½ sticks) unsalted butter, at room temperature
- 1 cup sifted powdered sugar, or a little more or less, depending on your taste
- ¼ teaspoon salt
- 1 tablespoon Vanilla Extract, homemade (page 165) or store-bought

---

how to frost a cake ~ Cut strips of parchment paper about 2 inches wide, and arrange the strips in a circle lining the outer rim of the cake stand or plate. Place one cake layer on top of the parchment strips—the parchment should cover the area between the cake and rim of the stand. Using an offset spatula (a spatula with a long metal end) or silicone spatula, create a very thin layer of frosting on the side of the cake and about 1½ inches on top of the cake. Center the second cake layer over the first, place it on top, and continue the thin layer of frosting on the top cake. Add the remaining frosting, smoothing the surface of the cake as you go. Remove the strips of parchment—your cake stand will be free of crumbs and errant frosting. A frosted cake will be okay for 1 day at room temperature.

---

variation ~ For chocolate frosting, add 4 ounces melted semisweet chocolate and 2 tablespoons unsweetened cocoa powder as you mix the frosting.

RIGHT AFTER JOEY AND I joined forces during our senior year in college, we took a road trip from Santa Fe to Vancouver. Our senior theses were behind us, and after a six-week diet of jellybeans and cigarettes, we were ready for a few cleansing weeks of road food. A road trip is a good thing for a new relationship, as a few thousand miles in the front seat of a car with someone is the ultimate test of compatibility. Luckily, we passed, and we still hop in the car for an hour here or there when we can't seem to connect any other way.

Anyone who has taken the Pacific Northwest tour probably knows that the region has a disproportionately vast amount of diners that are famous for their pie. Joey knew exactly where to take me, and honestly I don't remember eating anything on that trip besides pie. These diners had lengthy lists of berry varieties, meringues, and creams, and we'd scarf down the obligatory burger or omelet before moving on to the real reason we had come.

We had no idea that we would be married before the year's end, and that a year later from the day of our return, I would be waiting for my labor with Sadie to begin in our Massachusetts bedroom. We were just learning the first details about each other. At every stop, Joey ordered fruit pie and I ordered cream pie. In the hopes of bridging the gap between our tastes, we would take a token bite of the other's slice, but in the end, he had his fork, and I had my spoon.

Most people fall into one of two categories: pudding people and fruit people. As serious about his fruit pies as Joey is, I am passionate about pudding. And although a cream pie still brings me joy, I'm okay to dispense with the crust. When it's been a low week, or when I'm feeling off kilter, it's time to make pudding.

PUDDING SERVES 6 TO 7

- 4 cups whole milk
- ½ cup sugar
- ¼ teaspoon salt
- 1 vanilla bean, or 1 tablespoon Vanilla Extract, homemade (page 165) or store-bought
- ½ cup cornstarch

variation ~

CHOCOLATE PUDDING Omit the vanilla bean, reduce the sugar to ⅓ cup, and add 6 ounces roughly chopped bittersweet or semisweet chocolate or chocolate chips to the pudding when you would add the vanilla extract. Continue to stir and cook over medium heat until the chocolate melts into the pudding, 2 to 3 minutes.

1 Combine 3 cups of the milk with the sugar and salt in a heavy-bottomed medium saucepan and set it over medium-low heat. If you are using the vanilla bean, scrape out the seeds, put them in the milk, and add the whole bean. Heat until just steaming, stirring frequently.

2 In a small bowl or measuring cup, combine the cornstarch with the remaining 1 cup of milk. Stir well until the mixture is fairly lump free. Take the vanilla bean out of the pot and rinse it off. (Don't discard it—shove it into your homemade Vanilla Extract.) Raise the heat to medium-high. Add the cornstarch mixture and cook, stirring constantly with a wooden spoon, until the mixture just starts to bubble. Reduce the heat to low and stir continuously until the mixture thickens to something that looks like pudding and coats the back of the wooden spoon, 5 to 7 minutes. Add vanilla extract, if using. If the pudding is a bit watery, it's okay. It will thicken further as it chills.

3 Pour the pudding into individual dishes and chill for at least 3 hours before serving. If you have an aversion to pudding skin, press plastic wrap against the surface.

storage

FRIDGE • covered container or individual containers topped with plastic wrap, 2 to 3 days

FREEZER • no

tense moments ~ My pudding making usually looks something like this: Sadie scrapes the vanilla bean while Rosie gets cornstarch in her hair. They take turns stirring the pot, but then fight over whose turn it is, and in the process, the milk burns and ruins my favorite pot. A few tears are shed (sometimes mine), and I try to save the pudding while Sadie says it isn't her fault. This is how I acquired a taste for burnt pudding. So, if you'd like to make pudding with your kids, keep an eye on the pot. If making pudding alone, you can prevent scorching with focused stirring.

M Y FRIEND PAIGE might be wearing yoga pants and a hoodie, but underneath I think of her as all lipstick and cleavage— the classiest of '50s housewives. She is the kind of woman who hands me a drink as I hang up my jacket, whom I would smoke long and fancy cigarettes with in the kitchen if either of us smoked, and whose house everyone loves to walk into. Like many of us, she is torn between her home, work, family, and everything else. A childhood education from her mother's *Gourmet* magazines taught her to entertain and create a home like very few do, and when I asked her how she gets her head around the whole housewife thing, she let out something between a sigh and a laugh. "The feminist movement didn't liberate us from the kitchen. It told us we should be masters of the kitchen and the workplace and that we should do it all. It is, as I like to call it, a setup."

Many of us are looking into the past for answers to these questions. Grandmas are consulted, but so are their cookbooks, and in every kitchen there is an old community fundraising cookbook or a *Gourmet* cookbook from decades ago. Paige went to her mother's old cookbooks when I asked for a contribution to my growing recipe list. She was stuck on gelatin, as it was the only thing her children wanted to eat when they were under the weather. She figured that the ladies of the past would have lots of helpful advice on that most jiggly of refreshing desserts and comforting substances, but she came up empty. For housewives past, it was a *salad*, so all the gelatin recipes were in another chapter.

I don't eat gelatin very much, but I do love it. Although it will stay in the realm of the dessert around here, I am thankful to Paige, and to the women of the past, too, who were masters of comfort and home and just the right snack to soothe the belly and the soul.

FRUIT GELATIN

MAKES 4 CUPS, ENOUGH FOR 8 INDIVIDUAL ½-CUP PORTIONS

- 4 cups fruit juice (any will do—cranberry and peach are favorites)
- 2 envelopes (.5-ounce) unflavored gelatin
- *Optional:* 2 cups fresh, frozen, or canned fruit, such as blueberries, strawberries, grapes, or mandarin oranges

1   Pour 3 cups of juice into a medium saucepan and bring just to a boil over medium-high heat.

2   Pour the remaining 1 cup juice into a large mixing bowl and sprinkle the gelatin over the juice. Let it sit for 5 minutes, then pour the hot juice into the bowl and stir until the gelatin is completely dissolved.

3   If you are adding fruit, lay it on the bottom of the pan, mold, or individual dishes. Pour the liquid over the fruit and refrigerate, uncovered, until set, 6 to 8 hours.

storage
FRIDGE • covered containers, 3 days
FREEZER • no

I HAVE FINALLY COME AROUND TO VANILLA BEANS. The price always put me off, and so when a recipe called for vanilla beans, I always used the extract option that they put in there—you know, for the people who don't do the vanilla bean thing. But then I decided to give the beans a try, and I discovered the secret. Ten-dollar vanilla beans in little glass vials are not the way to go. Search online for "vanilla bean supplier" and you won't have to spend a fortune. Once you have a bag of vanilla beans in your pantry, the world opens up. Vanilla ice cream is flecked with lovely little black bits, pudding reaches a high point, and poached fruit becomes food for royalty. If you are at all like me in your secret thrill at small fancy things, it's an ingredient I would recommend.

Usually a recipe says to cut the bean lengthwise and to scrape the sticky paste of seeds into the milk or cream or what have you. Sometimes the bean gets thrown in as well. But then, the recipe always says to remove the bean and discard or save for future use. Future use? Shall I recycle it as a bracelet? Or a Christmas ornament? What recipe calls for a scraped and withered vanilla bean?

I'm so glad you asked.

Vanilla beans, powerful and lovely as they are, have quite a bit of strength in them. Scraped and withered they may be, but soaked in alcohol for a while, they create vanilla extract.

VANILLA EXTRACT YIELD VARIES

1 Fill a mason jar or bottle with vodka. After you use the seeds of a vanilla bean in a recipe, rinse off the vanilla bean and put it in the vodka. You'll need at least 3 vanilla beans in there for at least 3 weeks to get a good extract going, but it's fine to use more beans, too. Your extract is ready when it is a lovely brown color and it smells like vanilla.

2 Either pour the extract it into a new bottle and start over or keep topping off the working bottle with vodka and keep shoving more vanilla beans into the bottle. As long as you don't let it get too empty, you can keep using the extract indefinitely even as you continue to top it off.

- Cheap vodka, enough to fill your jar or bottle
- Spent vanilla beans, at least 3

storage
ROOM TEMPERATURE • sealed container, indefinitely

FREEZER • no

Carrots
$3.00 quart

frozen
vegetables

pizza

veggie burgers

chicken nuggets

fish sticks

ice cream
chocolate ice cream
strawberry ice cream
vanilla ice cream

frozen vegetables

IN MY TOWN, the farmers' market is not even 100 feet away from Town Hall—they are divided by a swath of railroad track, a patch of green, and an old gazebo. I spend a lot of time on that postage stamp of land—alternate Monday nights at Town Hall and most Saturday mornings at the market. Someone will have seen me in person or on public access television in my role as selectman, approving driveway permits or strategizing how to support new businesses. Then there I am the next morning, explaining the differences between purple and green scallions. The same person might have left the Monday meeting feeling victimized by his town government. But on Saturday he smiles at me and asks, "Do you know if I can freeze spinach?"

I talk about the difference between blanching and boiling, and how my friend Jen's method of freezing the bags flat makes stacking in the freezer so much easier. They walk away with a few pounds of spinach, excited to go home and store it for the winter. It's a smaller solution than they asked for on Monday, but a solution nonetheless.

Most vegetables can be frozen with great success—the method, however, changes with the type of vegetable. All vegetables should be frozen at peak freshness, as soon after harvest as possible. Label each freezer bag with the date and contents and press out any air. Spread the contents throughout the bag so you can stack and lay them flat in the freezer.

blanching

I recommend this technique for spinach, kale, chard, turnip and beet greens, mustards, collards, arugula (not the baby kind), and any other hearty green. The only greens that don't work this way are lettuce and cabbages. Blanching also works well to preserve corn, broccoli (and broccoli stems), peas (shelled and snap), and green beans. Prepare the vegetable as you would like to eat it by cleaning, stemming, shelling, or chopping.

Bring a large pot of water to a boil, and prepare another pot or mixing bowl with ice water. Plunge the prepared vegetable in boiling water for 15 to 30 seconds, then remove with a slotted spoon or small strainer and plunge into the ice water. Vegetables that are more tender, such as spinach and broccoli heads, require only 15 seconds, whereas heartier vegetables, like kale and broccoli stems, require closer to 30 seconds. Remove the vegetables from the ice water, squeeze out the excess liquid with your hands (especially in the case of greens), and store in freezer bags in portions that you would use in cooking (I store in 8-ounce amounts). Corn should be blanched on the cob for 30 to 45 seconds, then dropped in enough ice water to make sure the cob is cold (you might need to keep replenishing ice). Then cut the corn off the cob and freeze it in freezer bags. Frozen vegetables can be thawed or used right out of the freezer. During the winter, I put a small brick of greens into every soup.

roasting

Tomatoes, peppers, onions, and garlic can be roasted and stored together in bags for winter sauce. Roast peppers, onions, or garlic on trays in a 300°F oven for 1 hour. For roasting tomatoes, see page 96.

charring

This works for both hot and sweet peppers. Char peppers on the grill or under a hot broiler for about 5 minutes on either side, or until the skin is bubbled and black. Remove skins (use rubber gloves with hot peppers!).

raw freezing

Tomatoes can be frozen whole and raw, then thawed and cooked for sauce. Grated zucchini can be frozen raw and thawed for zucchini bread.

storage

Vegetables store well in the freezer for three to nine months, depending on the vegetable and the method. Frozen vegetables won't go bad—they'll just get a bit freezer-burned. Raw frozen tomatoes should be used within three months, whereas hearty greens such as broccoli stems last much longer, and everything else falls somewhere in between. Experiment in your own kitchen, but a well-stocked freezer will get you through a good portion of the winter.

PIZZA
—or—
the issue

WE HAVE A PIZZA ISSUE IN OUR MARRIAGE. Joey worked at Anthony's Pizza in Denver for nine years. He folded boxes there long before he was of legal working age, then worked in the kitchen and delivered pizzas as soon as he could get behind the wheel. If you took a cell sample from Joey when he was eighteen, you would find that he was about 88 percent pizza. It is part of his chemical makeup, but it is also the food of his soul.

I like all kinds of pizza, greasy or healthy. But when Joey was eating pizza all day long, I had my own limited diet. I was a picky kid, and for years, my mother made me noodles with broccoli and cheese on the side. My chemical makeup was more like 88 percent wheat, cheese, and broccoli. So you can guess what my favorite kind of pizza is.

Joey claims that the manager once threw a customer out of Anthony's for asking for broccoli on a pizza. He cheers as he tells this story.

Since I like to make food at home, I felt that pizza should be no exception. I made the dough, I made the sauce, and I even made the cheese. But when it came time to shape and top the crust, I fell apart and so did my dough. There were holes in the bottom and the whole mess had to be catapulted into the oven. I appealed to Joey. "Won't you make this right?"

"Pizza is like Chinese food. It should not be made at home."

That was a challenge if I had ever heard one. I dove into research, kneaded and fermented, and presented the results. Joey took a bite, and, deeply confused, finished his slice. I made it a few more times, and then one day when I pulled the dough from the fridge, he said, "Do you want me to make them?"

Success.

He made four little pizzas, each with my homemade sauce, homemade cheese, and our toppings of choice. Meat for Joey and Sadie, plain for Rosie, and for me? Well, I bet you can guess.

PIZZA MAKES 4 MEDIUM PIZZAS OR 6 SMALL PIZZAS

- 1¼ cups warm water
- 2 teaspoons active dry yeast
- 1 teaspoon sugar
- 2⅓ cups (11.65 ounces) unbleached all-purpose flour, plus additional for counter
- 1 cup (4.5 ounces) whole wheat flour (for added flavor, substitute ½ cup with rye flour)
- 1 teaspoon kosher salt
- 3 teaspoons olive oil
- 2 to 3 cups pizza sauce (see page 173)
- 1 pound Mozzarella, homemade (page 34) or store-bought
- Toppings (to your liking)

1 In a liquid measuring cup, combine the warm water, yeast, and sugar. Let stand for 5 minutes, or until there is a bit of foam on the surface of the liquid.

2 *If you are using a food processor,* combine the flours, salt, and 2 teaspoons of the olive oil in the bowl of the food processor and pulse to combine. With the machine running, add the yeast mixture as fast as the flour will absorb it. Process until the dough forms a ball and clings to the blade, then process for another 30 seconds. *If you are working by hand,* add the liquid slowly while kneading the dough in the bowl with the other hand, and then when the liquid is incorporated, knead on a floured surface for 5 minutes.

3 Use the remaining teaspoon of oil to grease a medium bowl and a piece of plastic wrap large enough to cover the bowl. Place the dough in the bowl, cover it with the plastic, and leave in a warm place to rise for at least 12 hours, but up to 24 hours. It will get nice and bubbly.

4 Preheat the oven to 475°F. With a bench knife or sharp knife, cut the dough into the desired number of pizzas. Shape the dough into a ball by gathering any loose ends under the ball. The underside of the ball can have a little gather, but the top should be smooth. Push the dough up in the center with your knuckles, shaping it into a dome while pinching the edges with your thumbs. Do this in a circular motion, letting gravity stretch the sides. As you press and pull, the sides will continue to expand. When the dough is about 8 inches in diameter, lay it on a floured surface and give it a few rolls with the rolling pin, starting from the center and moving outward. Then pick up the dough and resume your circular motion.

5 When the crust has reached the desired size and thinness and the oven is preheated, add the pizza sauce, mozzarella, and toppings.

AISLE 7

172

6   Bake the pizza on a pizza stone (see Note) or a baking sheet for 10 to 15 minutes, or until the sauce is bubbly and the crust is a little brown. If you are freezing the pizza, bake it for only 5 minutes.

storage

FRIDGE • dough, wrapped in plastic, 3 days

FREEZER • dough, cut into individual crust portions, wrapped in plastic and a freezer bag (thaw individual balls of dough in the refrigerator and shape when you are ready to make it). Or to freeze an entire pizza, bake for only 5 minutes. Let cool, wrap in one layer of plastic and one layer of aluminum foil. To eat the pizza, unwrap the layers and put the frozen pizza in a 475°F oven. Cook for 10 to 12 minutes, or until golden and bubbling. You can also freeze half-baked crusts and top them later. First, bake the crusts in a 475°F oven for 5 to 7 minutes, or until just hard to the touch. Let cool, then transfer to freezer bags. To serve, remove from the freezer, top crust with toppings, and bake in a 475°F oven for 10 to 12 minutes.

note ~ A pizza stone is a ceramic or stone tile that evenly distributes heat through the crust. Pizza stones are inexpensive and useful for other breads and baked goods as well. Preheat the stone with the oven.

---

pizza sauce ~ In a blender, combine one 28-ounce can of tomatoes, 2 tablespoons sugar, 1 teaspoon dried oregano (or 1 tablespoon fresh), 1 teaspoon dried basil (or 1 tablespoon fresh), $\frac{1}{2}$ teaspoon dried red pepper flakes, and 5 tablespoons tomato paste. Blend until smooth. Keeps in a covered container for up to 5 days in the refrigerator, or 6 months in the freezer.

---

tense moments ~ When Joey actually started helping me make pizza, I learned what I had been doing wrong. My primary mistake was putting sauce and toppings on the pizza long before it went into the oven, and this resulted in a soggy crust. Sauce and top each pizza just before it goes into the oven, and your crust will stay crisp.

VEGGIE BURGERS

—or—

the farm

gOULD FARM IN MONTEREY, MASSACHUSETTS, is a farm like many others in some respects—there are acres of organic gardens along both sides of the narrow road and cows that greet you with their kind stares. Up the hill there are pigs and chickens, and there is a dairy where Cheddar is cultured and aged before traveling to stores all over this part of the state. Poke your head into any door or walk through the garden beds and you will find staff and volunteers hard at work.

There are also "guests," residents who come to the farm for treatment of mental illnesses. Staff, volunteers, and guests work side by side, and often you will be hard-pressed to tell who fits into what role. It is a fully functioning farm and community, and there are so many success stories of people who have found their way to better health since the Farm began operations in 1913.

C. J. Walton came to Gould Farm as a volunteer in his early twenties. After a time at the Culinary Institute of America, he returned to the farm to develop his bread and pastry skills. He and the Harvest Barn team make bread, bagels, pastries, desserts, and yogurt for both the people who live and work at the Farm and the visitors who come to the café at the barn. I always end up talking to C. J. during my visits; whether it's his latest discovery on how to make ice cream more shelf stable or what new flour has improved the pizza crust; we get to talking and the girls always have to pull me out of there. C. J. also takes on the challenge of re-creating store-bought foods, and one Saturday I went into the café to buy croissants and I walked out with this recipe. If you are a veggie burger lover, try this one, and I'll wager that you'll never need another box of veggie burgers again. This comes together quickly, so have all of your ingredients chopped and ready to go.

VEGGIE BURGERS   MAKES EIGHTEEN TO TWENTY 5-INCH PATTIES

1 Heat the oil over medium heat in a large saucepan. Add the onion and cook until soft and shiny, about 3 minutes. Add the garlic, carrots, red pepper, and mushrooms and cook, stirring often, until soft and aromatic, about 10 minutes. Add the corn, cumin, oregano, chili powder, salt, and pepper. Continue to cook for 3 minutes more. Remove from heat and allow the mixture to cool slightly.

2 Preheat the oven to 425°F. In a large mixing bowl, combine 2 cups of the beans, 1 cup of the rice, and half of the cooked vegetable mixture. Mash with a potato masher until the ingredients are well blended. Use your hands to combine this mixture with the breadcrumbs, eggs, mustard, vinegar, soy sauce, yeast, and remaining 2 cups beans, remaining 1 cup rice, and cooked vegetables. Add the water chestnuts, if using. Let the mixture cool entirely.

3 Oil a baking sheet with olive oil. Using your hands, form the mixture into well-packed patties, about 4 inches in diameter. Lay the patties on the oiled baking sheet, and flatten with a spatula. Bake for 15 minutes, flip the patties, flatten with the spatula once again, and bake for another 15 minutes. Serve immediately, or if storing for later, allow to cool, then freeze on a baking sheet for at least 3 hours before transferring to freezer bags.

storage

FREEZER • freezer-safe container or bag, 4 months (microwave for 1 minute and then grill, or fry the frozen patties on low heat in a covered, oiled frying pan for 10 minutes on each side)

FRIDGE • (after defrosting) covered container, 4 days

- 2 tablespoons olive oil, plus extra for the baking sheet
- 1 medium onion, diced
- 6 garlic cloves, minced
- 2 medium carrots, shredded
- 1 red bell pepper, diced
- 10 large mushrooms, stems removed, caps diced
- ½ cup corn (fresh or frozen)
- ½ tablespoon ground cumin
- ½ tablespoon dried oregano
- ½ to 1 tablespoon chili powder, or to taste
- Salt and pepper, to taste
- 4 cups cooked Black Beans (page 99), from 2 cups dried black beans, or three 15.5-ounce cans black beans, drained
- 2 cups cooked short-grain brown rice (from 1 cup dry)
- 2 cups Breadcrumbs, homemade (page 223) or store-bought
- 2 large eggs, beaten
- 1 tablespoon Dijon mustard
- 2 tablespoons apple cider vinegar
- 2 tablespoons soy sauce
- 2 tablespoons nutritional yeast (see page 53)
- *Optional:* One 5-ounce can sliced water chestnuts, drained and roughly chopped

CHICKEN NUGGETS

—or—

at least it's protein

i'D VENTURE TO SAY that there are more chicken nuggets, tenders, and chicken fingers dipping into vats of hot oil than any other food at any given moment—it seems that those little crunchy bites provide sustenance for young picky eaters everywhere.

I have a friend who travels around the world with her daughter—she says it's a cinch since the adoption of the global kids' menu. Hong Kong? Geneva? Buenos Aires? For her five-year-old traveler there are always grilled cheese, hot dogs, quesadillas, and chicken nuggets. My friend has mixed feelings because she confesses that her daughter might be made mostly of cheese and breadcrumbs. And all her daughter learns about foods of other cultures is that chicken fingers are a universal language.

Of course, you don't always have to order off the kids' menu. You could splurge on a full-size entrée, or the kids could share one. But even if you could convince them that the *escargots* or *barbacoa* is exactly what they want, I promise you that the waitress will step in before they even order. "Would you like the quesadilla or the chicken nuggets?"

I'm going to give you a chicken nuggets recipe anyway. Because these things are never clear-cut. Because made in your own kitchen, chicken nuggets can be real food. And because in the end, sometimes we all just want to make a dinner that our kids will actually eat.

CHICKEN NUGGETS

1 Wash and dry the chicken breasts. Cut each breast into 2 × 2-inch pieces.

2 In a shallow bowl, combine the mayonnaise and lemon juice and stir until uniform. Combine the breadcrumbs, salt, and pepper in another shallow bowl. Set up your ingredients in a line: first the chicken on a plate or tray, then the mayonnaise mixture, then the breadcrumb mixture, then an oiled baking sheet. One at a time, dip each piece of chicken into the mayonnaise mixture, then the breadcrumb mixture, then set on the baking sheet. Refrigerate the tray of chicken for 20 minutes.

3 Preheat the oven to 375°F. Bake the chicken for 25 minutes, flipping the chicken pieces halfway through cooking.

storage

FRIDGE • covered container, 2 days (reheat in a 375°F oven or toaster oven for 8 to 10 minutes)

FREEZER • freezer-safe container or bag, 3 months (reheat directly from the freezer in a 375°F oven or toaster oven for 15 minutes)

- 1½ pounds boneless chicken breasts
- ½ cup Mayonnaise, homemade (page 117) or store-bought
- 1 teaspoon lemon juice (from ½ lemon)
- 3 cups Breadcrumbs, homemade (page 223) or store-bought
- 1 teaspoon salt
- Ground pepper
- Canola or olive oil for the baking sheet

i WAS SEVENTEEN YEARS OLD when I realized how easy it was to drive the three hours to the ocean from the hilly Berkshires. Alone or with friends, I would borrow my mother's car and trek over the wide Connecticut expanse to Misquamicut, Rhode Island. A morning in the car, a dive into the ocean, fried fish and a Coke, and I would be home by bedtime. The beach kept me sane that summer, and I made my way to college in New York that fall with sand in my hair and the perfume of fried fish lingering on my clothes.

A year later I was a college dropout on the other coast, and I walked through Golden Gate Park every morning to pay respects to the ocean before my first waitressing shift of the day. New York had spit me out and I had gone as far away as I could get, but I couldn't find the same comfort in the Pacific. I had assumed the oceans would be interchangeable, but they just were not. On my days off from the restaurant I would try the beach again at sunset, with the kissing couples and sun-salutating yogis.

I should have known I wasn't a Californian. I was born in San Francisco, but New England won out, and in the end what was really missing from those Pacific beaches was the smell of fried fish wafting through the air. There were oysters and hot dogs, but real fried indeterminate white fish was nowhere to be found. California and I did not last long.

I've always had a soft spot for store-bought fish sticks— with a bit of tartar sauce they are just enough like the seaside fried fish to make me crave them. Although the smell of fried fish on the beach has me sighing with satisfaction, it doesn't produce the same result in my kitchen, so I make these in the oven, and they are almost as good.

FISH STICKS   SERVES 6

- 2½ cups Breadcrumbs, homemade (page 223) or store-bought
- 1½ teaspoons salt
- ½ teaspoon paprika
- Ground pepper
- ½ cup all-purpose flour
- 1 pound white fish (cod, flounder, or anything similar), cut into 1-inch strips
- 2 large egg whites, lightly beaten
- Canola oil or cooking spray, for the wire rack

1 Combine the breadcrumbs, salt, paprika, and pepper in a mixing bowl. Pour the flour into a shallow bowl, and roll each strip of fish into the flour, then set it on a baking sheet to dry for 20 minutes.

2 Set out your workstation—it's really helpful to lay everything in a line on your counter. First comes the baking sheet with the fish, then the beaten egg whites in a second shallow bowl, then a heaping handful of the breadcrumb mixture in a third shallow bowl. At the end comes a wire rack, coated with canola or cooking spray. Put the rack onto an empty baking sheet. Take each piece of floured fish through the line—first in the egg, then the breadcrumb mixture, then onto the wire cooling rack. Refill the breadcrumb mixture from the mixing bowl when you need to, as once you get too much egg white into the mixture, it won't stick as well to the fish.

3 Preheat the oven to 350°F. Transfer the fish (on the rack, still nestled in the baking sheet) to the refrigerator for 20 minutes.

4 Remove the fish from the refrigerator and bake on the rack on the baking sheet for 12 to 15 minutes, or until the fish comes apart in flakes.

storage
FRIDGE • covered container, 1 day (reheat in a 350°F oven or toaster oven for 5 minutes)

FREEZER • freezer-safe container or bag, 3 months (reheat directly from the freezer in a 350°F oven or toaster oven for 10 minutes)

> **tartar sauce** ~ In a small bowl, combine 1 cup of Mayonnaise (page 117 or store-bought), 1 tablespoon fresh lemon juice, 1 chopped pickle, and 1 tablespoon capers. Season with salt and pepper to taste. Refrigerate for 1 hour before serving. Makes 1 cup.

eVERY JUNE, we make a pilgrimage to Thompson Finch Farm in Ancramdale, New York. Growing organic strawberries there is almost a religion, and arriving on a hot morning to acres of glistening strawberries, I can't help but fall to my knees and thank the God of summer. The girls dance and cheer around the perfect rows, stomping irreverently on the berries, staining their faces and clothes pink with the juice of the best fruit they've had since last year. Inevitably, I holler at them once or twice, "Respect the strawberries! Don't eat too many now!" We stuff our mouths with strawberries warm from the sun, and then we fill flats to take home to preserve. By the time we get home, all I can think about is fresh strawberry ice cream, possibly one of the best foods there is.

The moment you bring those strawberries in the door, this is your recipe. It will take just a little while to throw together, and after a few hours in the fridge and 20 minutes of churning, you will have your very own best strawberry ice cream. It's a perfect mix of fruit and cream inspired by a recipe from Alice Waters's classic *The Art of Simple Food* (Clarkson Potter, 2007). For the days when strawberries are not to be had, I offer two other classic ice creams adapted from David Lebovitz. If you find yourself addicted to throwing everything sweet into your ice cream maker (and I am!), his book *The Perfect Scoop* (Ten Speed Press, 2007) will become your manual. Top the ice cream with homemade hot fudge (see page 187) or spread between cake layers for homemade ice cream sandwiches, and you won't have to wait in line at the ice cream parlor.

CHOCOLATE ICE CREAM   MAKES 1 QUART

- 2 cups heavy cream
- 3 tablespoons unsweetened cocoa powder
- 5 ounces semisweet chocolate, chopped
- 1 cup whole milk
- ¼ cup sugar
- ¼ teaspoon salt
- 5 large egg yolks
- 1 teaspoon Vanilla Extract, homemade (page 165) or store-bought

1 Combine 1 cup of the cream and all the cocoa powder in a medium saucepan and bring to a low boil over medium heat. Whisk constantly as you heat the mixture to blend in the cocoa and prevent it from scorching. Let it boil as you whisk for 30 seconds, then remove from heat and whisk in the chocolate until completely smooth. Stir in the remaining 1 cup cream and scrape the mixture into a large mixing bowl. Set a fine-meshed sieve over the bowl.

2 Combine the milk, sugar, and salt in the saucepan (no need to wash it) and warm over medium heat just long enough to melt the sugar. Whisk the egg yolks together in a medium bowl, and add just a bit of the warm milk mixture into the yolks, whisking to temper the yolks. Then, very slowly, pour the rest of the milk into the yolks, whisking constantly. Pour the entire mixture back into the saucepan on medium heat and stir constantly with a wooden spoon, scraping the bottom and stirring until the mixture thickens and you get a good coating on the spoon or spatula. Pour the warm custard through the strainer, then stir it together with the chocolate mixture until smooth and uniform. Add the vanilla. Refrigerate, covered, for at least 3 hours before churning in your ice cream maker.

3 Freeze according to your ice cream maker's instructions.

> **tense moments** ~ Even though I have made many custard-based ice creams, my heart still beats fast as I watch for it to thicken. There are two things that can go awry here. The first is the possible scrambling of the eggs if they don't get tempered correctly. This is why you pour the custard over a strainer, to take out the chunks of cooked egg. The second is that the mixture might just not thicken enough. I have learned from experience that cursing at your wooden spoon for not having thick custard clinging to it does not help matters. If the custard is not custard-ing, go ahead and use it anyway. Your ice cream will be a bit less velvety, but ice cream is ice cream, and it will still be fabulous.

STRAWBERRY ICE CREAM MAKES 1 QUART

1 In a small bowl, whisk the egg yolks.

2 Place the half-and-half and ¼ cup of the sugar in a medium heavy-bottomed pot. Heat it over medium heat without letting it boil, and stir occasionally until the sugar is dissolved, 5 to 8 minutes. In the meantime, set a fine-meshed sieve over a large heatproof bowl.

3 When the half-and-half mixture is hot, whisk a little of it into the egg yolks to warm them. Then whisk all of the warm egg yolks into the hot cream. Stir constantly with a wooden spoon or heatproof spatula as you heat the mixture over medium heat—keep scraping the bottom and stirring until the mixture thickens and you get a good coating on the spoon. Again, *do not let it boil.* Remove from the heat and pour through the strainer over the bowl. Add the heavy cream to the mixture and stir to combine. Cover and chill in the refrigerator for at least 30 minutes.

4 Put the strawberries in a large bowl and mash them a bit with a potato masher. Then add the remaining ¼ cup sugar. Let the strawberries macerate in their own juices, stirring occasionally until the sugar has melted, 10 to 15 minutes. Add the berries to the cream mixture. Then add the vanilla, salt, and kirsch, if using. Chill, covered, in the refrigerator for at least 30 minutes, but up to 2 days.

5 Freeze according to your ice cream maker's instructions.

storage (all ice creams)

FRIDGE • unfrozen base, covered container, 2 days

FREEZER • ice cream, freezer-safe container, up to 5 days (thaw in the refrigerator for 20 to 30 minutes before serving)

- 3 large egg yolks
- ¾ cup half-and-half
- ½ cup sugar
- ¾ cup heavy cream
- 2 pints strawberries, washed, dried, and hulled
- 1 teaspoon Vanilla Extract, homemade (page 165) or store-bought
- ⅛ teaspoon of salt
- *Optional:* 2 teaspoons kirsch liqueur

VANILLA ICE CREAM MAKES 1 QUART

- 2 cups heavy cream
- ½ cup sugar
- ¼ teaspoon salt
- 1 vanilla bean
- 1 cup whole milk
- 1 teaspoon Vanilla Extract, homemade (page 165) or store-bought

1 Combine 1 cup of the heavy cream, the sugar, and the salt in a medium saucepan. Warm over medium heat, stirring to dissolve the sugar.

2 Cut the vanilla bean in half lengthwise and scrape the sticky seeds into the pan with a paring knife. Drop the bean into the pan. Remove from the heat, add the milk, remaining 1 cup cream, and vanilla extract to the pan. Stir to combine, then cover and refrigerate for at least 2 hours.

3 When you are ready to churn the ice cream, remove the vanilla bean, rinse it off, and put it into your Vanilla Extract. Freeze according to your ice cream maker's instructions.

ice cream sandwiches ~ Softened ice cream spread between your favorite cookies or graham crackers and then refrozen for a bit is really all you need to make it your own ice cream sandwich. But for those who, like me, have a deep attachment to the cake/cookie that frames the store-bought ice cream sandwich, Martha Stewart has found a way to re-create it:

Combine ½ cup melted butter with ½ cup sugar. Whisk in 1 large egg, 1 teaspoon Vanilla Extract (homemade, page 165, or store-bought), and ½ teaspoon of salt. Add ½ cup all-purpose flour and ¼ cup unsweetened cocoa powder and stir until thoroughly combined. Spread the batter into a 15 x 10-inch jelly-roll pan that you have buttered and lined with enough parchment paper so that there is an overhang on the 10-inch sides of the pan.

Bake in a 350°F oven for 10 minutes, or until the cake pulls away from the sides of the pan. Allow to cool completely while you soften 2 pints of ice cream. Lift the cake out of the pan using your parchment-paper handles, then cut it in half. Put one section of the cake on a large piece of plastic wrap, spread with softened ice cream, and top with the other section of cake. Wrap the entire large sandwich with plastic wrap and freeze for at least 2 hours. Remove from the freezer and cut into 8 sandwiches.

hot fudge ~ Set up a makeshift double boiler (see page 258). Bring the water to a simmer. Combine 6 ounces bittersweet chocolate, 4 tablespoons (½ stick) butter, ⅔ cup heavy cream, ¼ cup maple syrup, ¼ cup packed light brown sugar (homemade, page 51, or store-bought), ¼ cup unsweetened cocoa powder, and 1 teaspoon Vanilla Extract (homemade, page 165, or store-bought) in the bowl of your double boiler setup and stir the mixture as it sits over the steaming pot until it is smooth and lump free, 1 to 3 minutes. The fudge keeps in a covered container in the fridge for up to a month. To reheat, place container in a bowl of hot water and stir until softened, or reheat in a microwave.

8

pasta
and
sauce

pasta
pasta dough
ravioli

tomato sauce

pesto

macaroni
and cheese

lasagne

a T THE START of my sophomore year of college in Santa Fe, Eilen answered my ad for a roommate for the adobe house I had found a year earlier. Within a week, she reactivated the compost pile and planted fall greens in the abandoned raised beds out back. For our first Thanksgiving together, we made dinner for twenty. I had grown up with cooks all around me, but that holiday I came to the kitchen as my own person, separate from the kitchen standards of my mother and other adults who had fed me. Eilen refused to be intimidated by the hacking of a large pumpkin for pie or the careful folding of ravioli. If the recipe told her she could make it, then she was a believer, and she convinced me, too. With the gesture I would see again, Eilen shoved an issue of _Gourmet_ into my hand.

"Make ravioli!"

I didn't know who I would become in the next few years, but I knew it wouldn't be someone who made ravioli on the kitchen table again. I'd leave that to Eilen.

Eilen now travels the world with her guitar and drummer husband, and somehow she makes it here for every birthday. To most people she's a sultry voice in cowboy boots, but to Sadie and Rosie, she is Auntie E who spoils them at the toy store.

Although she's rarely home, Eilen's desire to cook for a crowd continues to overwhelm her. She confesses to having to check herself into a hotel when she needs to write songs; otherwise, the kitchen pulls her away. At my house she is likely weeding my garden or making potato rolls. And as I have planted my feet more firmly in the kitchen, she has cheered me on from wherever she is.

With every birthday comes a new kitchen tool in the mail from Eilen, and when I turned thirty, it was she who sent me a shiny silver pasta roller. Pasta rolling machines can work with two hands but are easier with four. When there is help in the kitchen, fresh pasta is the easiest thing in the world.

PASTA DOUGH MAKES JUST UNDER 1 POUND

THIS BASIC DOUGH is all you need for everything from spaghetti to lasagne to tortellini. Fresh pasta cooks much faster than dried, and most shapes will be ready in 2 minutes. Freshly made lasagna noodles go right into the pan without cooking.

1 Scoop the flour onto the counter and shape it into a volcano. Break the eggs into a bowl, pour them into the center of the volcano, and then beat the eggs with a fork, just incorporating the yolk and the whites. Use the fork to gently mix the flour into the egg mixture, working from the center out, maintaining the wall of the volcano as the center hole gets bigger. Don't be afraid of errant egg skating across the counter—just guide it back to the mix. When the egg is thoroughly incorporated, push the dough together into a ball and cover with a damp cloth or plastic wrap while you clean your hands and your work surface.

2 Unwrap the dough and place it on the clean counter and begin to knead it. It will come together! Vigorously push the dough down and away from you with one hand, and fold it over with the other for about 5 minutes, or until the dough has a smooth surface. Cut the dough into 6 pieces and shape each into a ball. Cover the balls of dough with plastic wrap and rest for 30 minutes.

3 *If using a pasta roller,* put one ball of dough through the roller at the thickest setting. Fold the strip in thirds, then put through again for a rectangle. Roll at the next thinnest setting, repeating until you have the desired thickness of pasta. For most pastas, you want to get the dough as thin as possible. *If using a rolling pin,* roll out each ball of dough, one at a time. To mimic the gradual thinning of the pasta roller, first roll to one thickness, then thinner, then thinner. Whether using a pasta roller or rolling pin, when the dough is $\frac{1}{16}$ of an inch, cut it to your preferred shape.

4 Hang the pasta to dry until you are ready to cook, at least 5 minutes, up to 2 hours. Make sure that pieces of pasta or dough do not touch as they dry, or they will stick together.

- 2 cups (10 ounces) all-purpose flour
- 3 large eggs

storage

FRIDGE • pasta dough, wrapped in plastic, 2 days; dried pasta wrapped into small nests, covered container, 2 days

FREEZER • first dried at room temperature for 1 hour, then in a freezer bag, 3 months (cook directly from the freezer)

PASTA AND SAUCE

RAVIOLI Makes thirty to thirty-five 2 x 3-inch ravioli

- 1 recipe Pasta Dough (page 191), at room temperature
- ¾ cup (6 ounces) Ricotta, homemade (page 26) or store-bought
- ¼ cup (.65 ounce) grated Parmesan cheese
- ¼ teaspoon salt, plus more for the cooking water
- Freshly ground pepper
- 1 large egg, lightly beaten
- Flour or cornmeal, for dusting the counter
- *Optional:* for filling, ¼ cup chopped fresh herbs such as parsley, basil, or sage; butter, oil, Tomato Sauce (page 195), or Pesto (page 197), for serving

THIS IS A GOOD FILLING to start you off, but please let your creativity take you wherever you like. Most combinations of meats and cheeses are lovely in this form, but fresh herbs, ground nuts, and pureed vegetables will work, too.

1   Roll out your pasta dough to the thinnest setting, and cut vertically into 6-inch-wide strips.

2   Combine the ricotta, Parmesan, salt, pepper, three-quarters of the beaten egg (keep reserved egg in a small bowl), and fresh herbs, if using, in a medium mixing bowl. Mix well. Dust the counter with flour or cornmeal. Lay a strip of pasta on the counter and scoop 1 teaspoon of filling onto the strip at about every 2 inches. Dip your finger in the remaining egg and use your fingertip to paint a circle around each scoop of filling. Fold the strip in half so that the filling is sealed and press the pasta around the filling to strengthen the seal.

3   Use a knife to cut the ravioli apart. Set your finished ravioli on parchment paper dusted with flour or cornmeal and allow to dry for at least 20 minutes.

4   Bring a large pot of salted water to a boil, then lower it to a medium simmer. Gently submerge the ravioli in the water and cook until they float to the surface, about 3 minutes. Drain, rinse, and reheat in the pot with butter, oil, or the sauce of your choice before serving.

storage

FRIDGE • covered container, 2 days

FREEZER • dried at room temperature for 1 hour, then in a freezer bag, 3 months (cook directly from the freezer)

variation ~ **TORTELLINI** Cut the sheets of pasta into 2½-inch circles with a small glass or biscuit cutter. (Let excess dough rest for 15 minutes under a dish towel before rerolling.) Spoon ⅛ teaspoon of filling into the center of each circle. Fold each circle in half and seal the semicircle by pressing the dough along the edge. Press your fingertip into the filled center. Gently bring the edges of the semicircle around to meet and press them together. Dry the finished tortellini on parchment dusted with flour or cornmeal for 20 minutes before cooking as directed. Makes 50 to 60 tortellini.

TOMATO SAUCE
—or—
rising and passing away

I N 2009, A LATE BLIGHT EPIDEMIC hit the tomato plants of the Northeast, and the region went into a panic. Customers marveled at the perfect heirloom tomatoes I was selling at the farmers' market for Indian Line Farm.

"You still have tomatoes."

"We do," I answered, and although I'm not a religious woman, a "God willing" snuck its way into my thoughts. The farmers, my friends Elizabeth and Al, and their small, devoted staff, planted and cared for those tomatoes. Week after week, Elizabeth and I worked the only stand left with overflowing bins of red, yellow, and green varieties of the prized fruit.

One morning, Elizabeth looked tired and worn, and I could tell that something had changed.

"I pulled them out yesterday. All of them."

The trademark brown spotted leaves led to doomed tomatoes, and to prevent spreading the blight to neighboring farms or home gardens, she had pulled hundreds of plants that were heavy with fruit. They couldn't even be composted, and she and Al buried the plants in the corner of their property like some forbidden contraband.

That morning, I watched Elizabeth as she explained the lack of tomatoes on the table. Returning customers reached across the table to hug her, apologizing as if there had been a death in the family. Elizabeth seemed to recover through the day, and the spiritual nature of the tomato and the farmer became more and more clear.

Fresh, frozen, or canned, I feel grateful for the tomato—for teaching me so much about the nature of things, and for agreeing so nicely to sauce up any occasion. This recipe is based on Marcella Hazan's classic tomato sauce with butter and onion from her *Essentials of Italian Cooking* (Knopf, 2002). The flavors come together to make a perfect product, and this couldn't be easier to make.

TOMATO SAUCE MAKES 3½ CUPS

1 Combine the tomatoes, onion, garlic, and butter in a medium saucepan. Bring to a boil over medium-high heat, then cover, reduce the heat to low, and simmer for 30 minutes, stirring occasionally to prevent scorching and to break up the tomatoes. Remove the onion and garlic and either compost or eat separately (they will be wonderfully sweet). Add the salt and oregano and then adjust the salt to taste.

2 If you prefer a smooth sauce, use your immersion blender to whir out any chunks. For an even smoother sauce, blend first, then pass through a food mill.

storage

FRIDGE • covered container, 5 days

FREEZER • freezer-safe container, 6 months

CANNABILITY • no

variation ~ In the late summer, when the tomatoes are plentiful, you can whip up a quick fresh sauce. Sauté 1 minced onion and 4 minced garlic cloves in 2 tablespoons of unsalted butter or olive oil. Add a few sprigs of fresh oregano and rosemary, if you have them. Core and chop 2 pounds of tomatoes and add them to the mix. Cover and cook on low heat for 15 minutes, stirring occasionally. Finish with fresh basil and salt and pepper to taste.

- One 28-ounce can whole tomatoes; or 1 quart Canned Tomatoes, homemade (page 97) or store-bought; or 2 pounds Roasted Tomatoes for the Freezer (page 96), thawed in the refrigerator (include any liquid from the can or bag)

- 1 medium onion, halved, peeled but not chopped

- 3 garlic cloves, peeled but not chopped

- 6 tablespoons (¾ stick) unsalted butter, or 6 tablespoons olive oil

- 1 teaspoon salt, plus more to taste

- 1 teaspoon dried oregano

PESTO
—or—
bitter coffee and stale croissants

hOW MANY terrible coffee shops do we endure in our lives because of Wi-Fi, location, allegiance to friends, or any other assortment of reasons?

The world is peppered with perfect coffee shops—sunlit wooden havens with comfortable chairs and music at the perfect volume that creates your very own soundtrack. These coffee shops serve coffee that tastes better than our morning homemade cup. We love the wide mugs and the harmonic tone of the milk steamer echoing off the walls. Nothing is venti or grande—there is just small and large, and maybe medium. We walk into these shops and decide we want to move to this or that town, just to be repeat customers.

Unfortunately there are more bad coffee shops than perfect ones. The baked goods are dry and tasteless, the coffee is bitter, and the place smells like dirty mop water. Yet we return.

Long before Joey ambled into my life, I spent far too much time at one such place in pursuit of the affection of a man who swore it was the only coffee shop for him. One could perhaps call it a relationship, but really he would show up in the random corners of my life and I found excuses to frequent his favorite places. I'd study at the little coffee shop that claimed his loyalty even though I hated the place. I had to find another excuse to keep returning, and so I went through every item on their menu. Finally, their bagel, toasted with cream cheese and served with a side of pesto, was a taste revelation for me. The pesto was oily and green, and my heart would flip with the first luscious bite. The relationship didn't last, but the pesto stayed in my heart, and to this day the bagel/pesto/cream cheese combination is still one of my favorite things to eat.

Because pine nuts can be pricy, I re-create that pesto with blanched toasted almonds. Substitute pine nuts if you have a cup or two—just keep a few of them whole and stir them in at the end.

PESTO   MAKES 1 CUP

1 Combine the garlic and almonds in a food processor and pulse a few times to chop. Add the lemon juice and basil leaves, and process until the basil is finely minced.

2 Add the olive oil and salt and process again for a few seconds. If freezing the pesto, stop here. Otherwise, add the Parmesan with a final pulse. Taste and adjust the salt as needed.

storage

FRIDGE • covered container, topped with olive oil, 3 days

FREEZER • in freezer-safe container before adding cheese, topped with olive oil, 6 months (thaw in refrigerator and add Parmesan cheese before serving)

- 2 garlic cloves, minced
- ½ cup (2 ounces) blanched, slivered almonds, lightly toasted
- 1 teaspoon fresh lemon juice (from ¼ lemon)
- 2 cups packed fresh basil leaves, washed, dried thoroughly, and roughly chopped
- ½ cup olive oil
- ½ teaspoon salt, plus additional to taste
- ½ cup grated Parmesan cheese

bAKED MACARONI AND CHEESE, the kind with cream sauce and breadcrumbs and a whole brick of cheese, is for births and deaths and breakups and other transitions that wrench or elevate the soul. For me, there is nothing else that will quite do the trick.

I lived on homemade stovetop mac and cheese for the first decade of my life. Boiled noodles rewarmed in butter and cheese and a little milk was all I required, and whether homemade or from a box, it brings joy to almost everyone. I ate my first baked mac and cheese when I returned home from my freshman year at boarding school to say goodbye to my grandmother. At sixty-six, she had run her blue Buick into a dump truck in the opposite lane on a country road, and by the time I got home she was in a coma. The family gathered around my grandmother's table so that we could, in the words that she would have used, eat a little nosh and regain our strength. My aunt Cindy, the oldest child who took the care of the family onto her shoulders, made a dense and steaming pan of mac and cheese, and we sat around it like it was an altar. My grandmother died that weekend, and I think it was that mac and cheese that gave us the strength to carry on through the week that followed.

Whenever I hear that someone might need such a meal, I start boiling water for the noodles. I throw the butter in the pot to get the cream sauce going, and I check to make sure that I have a big brick of cheese in the fridge. Whenever the soul needs a little glue to hold it together, there is always mac and cheese.

MACARONI AND CHEESE   SERVES 6 TO 8

- Salt
- 1 pound penne, macaroni, or shells
- *Optional:* 1 medium head of broccoli, cut into bite-size pieces (including the stem)
- ¼ cup (½ stick) unsalted butter, plus additional for the pan
- 4 cups whole milk
- 6 tablespoons all-purpose flour
- 1 teaspoon paprika (sweet or smoked), plus additional for sprinkling over the top
- 1 teaspoon dry mustard
- Freshly ground pepper to taste
- 1 pound grated Cheddar cheese, or a mix of Cheddar and Gruyère
- 2 cups Breadcrumbs, plain or garlic, homemade (page 223) or store-bought

1 Bring a large pot of salted water to a rolling boil over high heat. Add the pasta and cook for half the time specified on the package. Add the broccoli, if using. Cook for another 2 minutes and drain and rinse in cold water. Set aside.

2 Preheat the oven to 350°F. Grease a 9 × 13-inch baking pan with butter.

3 Bring the milk just to a boil in a medium saucepan and set aside. Meanwhile, melt the butter in another medium saucepan. Add the flour and whisk over low heat just until the mixture turns golden and fragrant, about 2 minutes. Add the hot milk to the flour mixture and whisk well. Add the paprika and dry mustard and continually whisk over medium heat until the mixture thickens, about 5 minutes. Season the mixture with salt and pepper to taste.

4 Pour the penne and broccoli into the baking dish. Pour the cream sauce over the pasta and toss to coat completely. Sprinkle three-fourths of the cheese on top, then all of the breadcrumbs, then the remaining cheese. Finish with a little extra paprika and some salt and pepper. Bake for 30 minutes, or until golden and starting to bubble. Then put it under the broiler for a few more minutes, until it puffs up and turns an even darker golden. Allow it to sit for 10 minutes before serving.

storage

FRIDGE • covered with plastic wrap or aluminum foil, 4 days (reheat, covered, in a 350°F oven)

FREEZER • whole and unbaked, wrapped in aluminum foil (thaw in refrigerator before baking); baked, in the pan wrapped in aluminum foil, or in individual portions in freezer-safe containers, 4 months (thaw and warm in a microwave or on the stovetop)

tense moments ~ Keep whisking—your sauce will thicken! The key is to cook the flour gently without too much browning. Add the hot milk and stir until it thickens—it will eventually happen. Even if it doesn't seem thick enough, use it anyway. It will come together as it bakes. A thinner sauce will also do fine here.

I HAND ROSIE A PLATE with a perfect piece of lasagne. I admire it as I pass it across the table, but she holds her nose. "Blech. I want plain noodles."

I know where Rosie's coming from. I liked at least a clean inch of space between ingredients when I was a kid. I demanded a new fork after finishing my noodles and before starting my broccoli.

I don't know why I try—my argument has never worked before. "Rosie, it's all the things you love. Noodles, cheese, sauce. That's all."

"I want plain noodles. Put the sauce and the cheese on the side."

I don't know how the taste buds grow up, but I know that one day I started to love perfect elements in combination. I have faith that Rosie will find her way—that she, too, will find revelation in the marriages of elements, that she will discover those flavors that come together with a rush on her tongue.

I can't help but wonder what she will love.

I love eggs and sauerkraut. Quince and cheese. Tarragon and potato. Silky noodles with ricotta and mozzarella and tomato sauce. I love that most of all.

When you are preparing to bring together these elements into just the right marriage, it is a good idea to keep a few principles in mind. Balance is important, and too many noodles will create a mush of wheat and cheese. Stick to the order in the recipe, and don't skimp on the sauce and filling. With enough love and cheese, your lasagna will always come together in the perfect combination.

LASAGNE   SERVES 8

- 1 recipe Pasta Dough (page 191), in sheets, or 1 pound dried store-bought lasagna noodles

- 1 teaspoon salt, plus additional for pasta water if using store-bought noodles

- 2 cups (1 pound) Ricotta, homemade (page 26) or store-bought

- 2 large eggs, beaten

- ¼ teaspoon ground pepper

- ½ teaspoon grated nutmeg

- 3½ to 4 cups Tomato Sauce, homemade (page 195) or store-bought

- 1 pound Mozzarella, homemade (page 34) or store-bought, sliced into ¼-inch-thick rounds

- ¾ cup grated Parmesan cheese

1   Preheat the oven to 375°F if baking the lasagne now. If using store-bought noodles, cook them in boiling salted water for 5 minutes. If using homemade noodles, you can roll them out as you assemble the lasagne so they go straight from the roller to the pan, cutting the pasta to fit as you go.

2   Combine the ricotta, eggs, salt, pepper, and nutmeg in a medium bowl and thoroughly combine.

3   Spoon ½ cup tomato sauce into a 9 × 13-inch baking pan and spread around the pan. Cover with a layer of noodles. Evenly lay several spoonfuls of ricotta mixture over the noodles. Add a third of the remaining sauce, half the mozzarella, and another third of the noodles. On top comes the rest of the ricotta mixture, a third of the sauce, then the rest of the mozzarella. Top with the remaining noodles, the rest of the sauce, and all of the Parmesan.

4   Cover with aluminum foil, making a tent so the foil does not touch the cheese. If freezing the lasagne, transfer it to the freezer now. Otherwise, bake for 40 minutes, then remove the aluminum foil and bake for 15 more minutes, or until is the sauce is bubbling and the top is golden. Allow to sit for 10 minutes before serving.

storage

FRIDGE • covered with plastic wrap or aluminum foil, 3 days

FREEZER • whole and unbaked, wrapped in aluminum foil (thaw in refrigerator before baking); baked, in the pan wrapped in aluminum foil, or in individual portions in freezer-safe containers, 4 months (thaw and warm in a microwave or on the stovetop)

variations ~ As long as there is some balance of ingredients, there is an endless possibility of combination. Pesto is a wonderful addition, and cut tomato slices can replace tomato sauce. Add ground beef, sausage, or veal to the sauce. Spinach can be folded into the filling. Butternut squash puree can stand in for tomato sauce, especially with the addition of sage and browned butter.

AISLE

9

breads and crackers

hamburger buns

sandwich bread
wheat bread
white bread

tortillas
corn tortillas
flour tortillas

graham crackers

breadcrumbs

breadsticks

crackers
wheat crackers
cheese crackers

i FIND THAT I NOW DO SO MANY THINGS that I didn't used to do. For example, I enjoy math. I read comic books on occasion. I garden. I know how to can a jar of preserves. I will sing karaoke after a drink or two. I have been to Morocco. I am not afraid of yeast.

Yeast and I are still building our relationship. I've made a few dense loaves of bread that would break a glass coffee table if dropped from a certain height. I have been known to talk to my yeast, "Froth, God damn it, aren't you alive?" only to kill it with anger. "Rise to double its bulk" doesn't always jibe in my kitchen.

These buns helped me believe in the power of yeast. They rise every time. And now I'm ready to say that I'm someone who makes bread.

These are fabulous hamburger buns. I started with a recipe in the *New York Times,* from Hidefumi Kubota of Comme Ça in Los Angeles and then I played with it until it was easy enough for me to make on impulse. The buns are lighter than most and sweet in a way that goes really well with a pickle. They come together quickly, and I think you'll hesitate going back to store-bought buns after the first bite.

HAMBURGER BUNS

—or—

adjusting your self-identity

HAMBURGER BUNS   MAKES 8 BUNS

- **1 cup warm water (about 110°F)**
- **3 tablespoons whole milk**
- **2 teaspoons active dry yeast**
- **2 tablespoons sugar**
- **3 large eggs**
- **3¾ cups (1 pound, 2.75 ounces) all-purpose flour, plus additional for the counter**
- **1½ teaspoons salt**
- **2½ tablespoons unsalted butter, at room temperature**
- ***Optional:* poppy, sesame, or caraway seeds, coarse salt**

note ~ I don't care if you only have a glass pan, do not use it for this purpose! If the pan stays filled with hot water throughout, the glass will be okay. But if (hypothetically) the water evaporates and you refill it, and if (not quite thinking straight) you pour cold water in your hot glass pan (I know! You can already see how this is going to end), the pan will not so hypothetically explode, propelling shards of glass through your kitchen and at your children, who will then refuse to put on shoes while you cry and pick glass out of your hamburger rolls. Just use the metal pan.

1 In a liquid measuring cup, combine the warm water, milk, yeast, and sugar. Let stand until foamy, about 5 minutes. Meanwhile, beat 2 eggs in a small bowl.

2 In a large bowl, whisk the flour with the salt. Add the butter to the flour and gently rub it in with your fingers. Stir in the yeast mixture and beaten eggs until the dough starts to come together.

3 Dump the dough onto a well-floured counter and knead vigorously, folding the dough onto itself and throwing it down onto the counter. Work with it for about 10 minutes, adding additional flour when the dough gets sticky. Shape the dough into a ball and return it to its bowl. Cover with plastic wrap and let the dough rise in a warm place until doubled in bulk, about 2 hours.

4 Line a baking sheet with parchment paper. Using a knife, divide the dough into 8 equal parts. Gently roll each part into a ball and arrange 2 to 3 inches apart on a baking sheet. Cover loosely with a clean dish towel and let the buns rise in a warm place for 1 to 2 hours.

5 Preheat the oven to 400°F with the rack in the center. Fill a metal pan with water and set it on the oven floor or bottom rack (see Note).

6 In a small bowl, beat the remaining egg with 1 tablespoon of water and brush some of the mixture on top of the buns with a pastry brush. If you are using seeds and/or coarse salt, sprinkle them over the egg wash. Place the buns in the oven and bake, turning the sheet halfway through baking, until the tops are golden brown, about 20 minutes. Transfer to a rack to cool completely.

storage
ROOM TEMPERATURE • covered container or sealed bag, 2 days
FREEZER • cut in half lengthwise, freezer bag, 6 months

n INETEEN YEARS AFTER SHE GAVE BIRTH TO ME, my mother met a Canadian architect with a big heart and became a mother again. I was at Maia's birth, and I knew I would have a certain responsibility to this baby. As an adult, I was also a friend to my mother and different kind of sister to Maia.

I became a parent a few years later, and what could have been two families became one. Four parents to three children is a pretty good ratio, and we work together in the roles that suit us. When there is a musical at the local theater, my mother takes them. When flour and yeast are in the mix, the work is mine.

When King Arthur Flour visited Maia's sixth-grade class, they sent her home with a bag of flour and a bread-baking assignment due the next day. My mother called me in a panic, and I knew this was one of those times I could parent my sister.

I talked Maia through proofing the yeast, and she read me the recipe over the phone. Bread, I told her, wanted to be made. All it needed was a gentle mix and guidance from her hands and dough would do its own work.

When we are in the kitchen together I always try to pull Maia over to whatever bowl I'm stirring, to show her how to melt chocolate or how to fold egg whites into a batter. She's a baker—I can see it, and I do my best to step in when I'm needed.

Basic bread is one of the most satisfying staples to make at home—get into a routine and you'll never pay for bread again. Here are two different breads: wheat and white. The wheat bread recipe is inspired by Peter Reinhart's Everyday 100% Whole-Wheat Sandwich Bread from his beautiful book *Artisan Breads Every Day* (Ten Speed Press, 2009), and although there is a bit of a time commitment, your final loaves will be so wonderful. The white bread recipe is based on King Arthur Flour's White Bread 101 from *The King Arthur Flour Baker's Companion* (Countryman Press, 2003). It comes together quickly, will please the white bread lovers in your life, and slices like a dream.

WHEAT BREAD   MAKES 2 LOAVES

- 6¼ cups (28 ounces) whole wheat flour, plus additional for the dough (if needed) and the counter
- 1 tablespoon kosher salt
- 5 tablespoons (2.5 ounces) packed light brown sugar, homemade (page 51) or store-bought
- 1 large egg
- ¼ cup canola oil, plus additional for greasing the bowl and the loaf pans
- 1¼ cups lukewarm (90°F to 100°F) water
- 1¼ cups lukewarm (90°F to 100°F) whole or 2% milk or whey (see page 26)
- 1½ tablespoons dry active yeast

1 Whisk together the flour, salt, and brown sugar in the bowl of a stand mixer or a large mixing bowl. In a small bowl, whisk together the egg and canola oil, then combine the lukewarm water and milk in a separate small bowl. Check the mixture with the thermometer to make sure it's at the right temperature, then whisk in the yeast until it is mostly dissolved. Add both the egg and milk mixtures to the dry ingredients.

2 *If using a mixer*, fit it with the paddle attachment and mix on low speed for about 1 minute. Stop the mixer and let the dough sit in the bowl for 5 minutes. Change to the dough hook and mix on medium-low speed for 2 minutes. The dough should be slightly elastic and a bit sticky. If it feels really wet, add 1 or 2 tablespoons of flour, and if it is so hard that your mixer is stressed, add 1 or 2 tablespoons of room temperature water. Continue to mix with the dough hook for another 4 minutes, increasing the speed for the last few seconds. Turn the dough out on a lightly floured counter. *If mixing by hand*, follow the same timing and texture recommendations as the mixer instructions. Use a large wooden spoon and mix vigorously, making sure to incorporate all of the flour and beat up the dough as you stir.

3 Knead the dough a few times, then do what Peter Reinhart calls a "stretch and fold"—reach under the front end of the dough, stretch it out, then fold it onto the top of the dough. Now repeat from the back end of the dough, as well on each side. Flip the dough, shape it into a ball, cover with a clean, damp dish towel, and let sit for 10 minutes. Repeat the stretch and fold process, cover, and let it rest for another 10 minutes. Stretch and fold one more time and let it rest for 10 minutes.

4 Lightly grease a large mixing bowl, place the dough into it, and cover tightly with plastic wrap. Refrigerate for at least 24 hours, and up to 3 days. Over time, you will probably see bubbles in the dough—this is the fermentation that will give the bread its flavor.

5 Remove the dough from the refrigerator 3 hours before you bake. Turn it out on a lightly floured counter and divide it into 2 equal pieces. Shape each piece into a sandwich loaf by flattening it out into a rectangle about 5 × 8 inches. Starting with the narrow side of the rectangle, roll it up into a log. Pinch the seam closed and give the log a few rolls on the counter to even it out. Make sure that the shape is fairly regular, and that the ends of the log aren't narrower than the center. Place the logs into two greased 8½ × 4½-inch loaf pans, cover loosely with plastic wrap, and allow to rise at room temperature for 2 to 3 hours, or until the dough is 1 inch above the rim of the pan.

6 Preheat the oven to 350°F when the dough looks almost ready to bake. Remove the wrap and bake the loaves in the center of the oven for 40 to 50 minutes, turning the pans halfway through baking. They are done when the tops are golden brown and sound hollow when tapped. Turn the pans to release the loaves immediately and let cool on a wire rack for at least 1 hour before cutting.

storage

ROOM TEMPERATURE • paper or plastic bag, 4 days
FREEZER • sliced, in freezer bags, 4 months

tense moments ~ Remember that yeast is a living thing. There is always a chance that it could be old and inactive. If there is no sign of foam when you mix your yeast with the liquid, then throw it out and start with new yeast. Rising times will vary depending on your kitchen, so go on how it looks, as opposed to how long it has been sitting. Most of all, if you are new to baking with yeast, relax. My friend Hedley swears that the yeast responds to stress in the people who are working with it. Try to get into the feel of the dough and the process of the recipe, and if things don't work the way you want them to, the worst that can happen is that your bread is a little dense.

WHITE BREAD   MAKES 2 LOAVES

- 6 cups (1 pound, 14 ounces) all-purpose flour, plus additional for the dough (if needed) and the counter
- 4 teaspoons instant yeast
- 2½ teaspoons salt
- 6 tablespoons sugar
- ½ cup (1 stick) unsalted butter, melted
- ½ cup nonfat dry milk powder
- 2¼ cups lukewarm (90°F to 100°F) water
- Vegetable or olive oil for the counter, loaf pan, and plastic wrap

1   *If using a mixer,* combine the flour, yeast, salt, sugar, melted butter, dry milk powder, and lukewarm water in the bowl of the mixer. Using the dough hook, knead on medium-low speed until the dough comes together and becomes soft, smooth, and pliable, 5 to 7 minutes. If it feels really wet, add 1 or 2 tablespoons of flour, and if it is so hard that your mixer is stressed, add 1 or 2 tablespoons of room temperature water. *If mixing by hand,* combine ingredients in your largest mixing bowl. Stir with a wooden spoon until the dough starts to come together. then shift to your hands and knead the dough in the bowl until you have a soft, smooth, and pliable dough.

2   Cover the bowl with a clean, damp dish towel and let it rise for about 1 hour. It will not necessarily double in bulk, but it will puff up a bit, so go by the timing instead of the look of it.

3   Spread a thin layer of oil on the counter, rubbing off any excess. Lightly grease two 8½ × 4½-inch loaf pans as well. Transfer the dough to the counter, divide it into two equal parts, and roll each into an 8-inch log in the method outlined for Wheat Bread (page 213). Lay the dough into the prepared pans, cover lightly with greased plastic wrap, and let rise until the dough is 1 inch above the rim of the pan, about 1 hour.

4   Preheat the oven to 350°F when the dough looks almost ready to bake. Remove the plastic wrap and bake the loaves in the center of the oven for 30 to 40 minutes, turning the pans halfway through baking. The loaves are done when the tops are golden brown and sound hollow when tapped. Turn over the pans to release the loaves immediately and let them cool on a wire rack for at least 1 hour before cutting.

storage

ROOM TEMPERATURE • paper or plastic bag, 2 to 3 days

FREEZER • sliced, in freezer bags, 4 months

t HERE ARE JUST A FEW SMALL, simple necessities that cause riotous panic when absent from the kitchen. Butter. Coffee. Tortillas.

When Joey and I moved to New England after college in New Mexico, there was some tension around the tortilla issue. Joey was from Denver, but I, being the newly pregnant one, pulled us eastward back to my mother and stepfather, who would soon be grandparents. Joey grew a beard, got himself some muck boots, and immediately found joy in the best attributes of his newfound home: fireflies. Real maple syrup on every pancake. A drive that ends in the ocean. The lack of decent tortillas, however, was a serious issue.

While in New Mexico, I, too, had become dependent on the tortilla. The desert had worked its way into my heart and belly. Green chile would continue to spice my dreams, and I would have to accept that, but tortillas? How hard was it really to make a good tortilla? It turns out, not so hard at all.

CORN TORTILLAS MAKES TWELVE 6-INCH TORTILLAS

- 2 cups masa harina (lime-treated cornmeal, available at Latin grocers and many supermarkets)

ALTHOUGH IT MIGHT SEEM LIKE AN EXTRANEOUS GADGET to acquire, I recommend that you seek out a tortilla press if corn tortillas are a staple in your kitchen. A fancy wooden one that you might find in a restaurant is nice, but a silver-painted cast-iron one will do the trick, too. Flour tortillas will roll out nicely with your rolling pin, but corn tortillas not so much. A tortilla press produces a nice flat and, most important, circular tortilla that pleases everyone, even my displaced westerner husband.

1   Combine the masa harina and 1¼ cups water in the bowl of a stand mixer or a mixing bowl. *If using a stand mixer,* use the dough hook and mix for 1 minute, or until the dough comes together in a ball. *If mixing by hand,* mix and knead the dough with your hands in a bowl until the dough comes together. Shape the dough into 12 balls, each about 3 inches in diameter. Lay a clean, damp dish towel over the balls of dough while you press the tortillas.

2   Start a cast-iron skillet or griddle, ungreased, over medium heat on the stove.

3   Line each side of the tortilla press with half a large freezer bag separated along the seam. Place a ball of dough in the center of the press and close it with all your weight. Open the press and peel the tortilla off the plastic. Transfer the tortilla to the heated griddle and cook for 30 seconds to 1 minute on each side, or until little spots appear on the surface. Use the spatula to remove the tortilla from the pan. Repeat with the other balls of dough. Serve immediately, or store, covered, in a warm oven or under a warm, damp cloth until ready to serve.

storage

FRIDGE • covered container or freezer bag (reheat in a dry skillet over medium heat)

FREEZER • freezer bag, 3 months (thaw in the fridge and reheat in dry skillet over medium heat)

shortening and lard ~ I don't use shortening or lard in my recipes very much, but when it's necessary, as in flour tortillas and filling for Sandwich Cookies (page 276), there are some great options out there. Earth Balance makes a nonhydrogenated vegetable shortening that works well, and it won't do the same damage to your arteries as the stuff in the plastic tub from your childhood. Look for locally farmed lard at your farmers' market or through a farmer in your area.

make your own tortilla chips! ~ Cut homemade or store-bought tortillas (wheat or corn) into triangular wedges. Fry the wedges in a deep fryer or skillet with 2 inches of oil heated to 375°F, until the chips are puffed and crispy, about 10 minutes. Lay them on a paper towel to drain and toss with coarse salt.

FLOUR TORTILLAS MAKES SIXTEEN 8-INCH TORTILLAS

- 4 cups (1 pound, 4 ounces) all-purpose flour, plus additional for the counter

- 2 teaspoons salt

- 1 teaspoon baking powder

- 2 tablespoons unsalted butter, cut into ½-inch pieces

- 4 tablespoons (2 ounces) nonhydrogenated vegetable shortening or lard, cut into ½-inch pieces (see page 217)

storage

FRIDGE · covered container or freezer bag (reheat in a dry skillet over medium heat)

FREEZER · freezer bag, 3 months (thaw in the fridge and reheat in dry skillet over medium heat)

THE SECRET (ISN'T IT ALWAYS?) is a good amount of fat blended into the dough. I often use a combination of butter and nonhydrogenated vegetable shortening, but if you have access to good-quality lard, that will be fabulous, too. These are classic tortillas, and as they puff in your skillet you'll see the resemblance to so many other flatbreads from other cultures—you can use this as a naan bread with your Indian food as well. You don't need a tortilla press for wheat tortillas; a rolling pin will work better here. The dough is a bit sticky, but just flour the dough as you roll it.

1   Combine the flour, salt, and baking powder in a large mixing bowl. Add the butter and shortening, and rub them into the flour mixture with your hands until you have pea-size lumps. Slowly add 1½ cups of warm water to the mixture, tossing with your hands as you go. Add an additional 1 tablespoon of water at a time (but don't use more than 4 additional tablespoons) until you have a slightly sticky dough. Lay a clean, damp dish towel over the bowl. Let the dough rest for 10 minutes.

2   Flour the counter and divide the dough into 16 balls, each about 3 inches in diameter. Cover the balls with the damp towel and let rest for 5 minutes. Start heating a dry skillet on the stove over medium-high heat. (If you have two skillets, use them both.)

3   Use the rolling pin to roll out your first tortilla to 8 inches in diameter and 1/16 inch thick. Put it in the skillet and cook for 1 minute on each side, or until it is bubbly and starting to brown. Use the spatula to remove the tortilla from the pan. Repeat with the other balls of dough. Serve immediately, or store, covered, in a warm oven or under a warm, damp cloth until ready to serve.

JOEY STARTED TEACHING PRESCHOOL when Sadie was three years old, and he and Sadie started school the same September. Rosie wasn't far behind, and now the three of them cheerily pile into the car together in the morning, and they grumpily tumble out of it together in the afternoon. I have worked so many jobs in the past few years that fill the hours in between, but I do my best to be there for Joey and the girls at 4:00, when it's possible. I never imagined myself in the kitchen with an apron and a plate of warm cookies, but if there is a good moment to find my inner housewife, this is it. Car Snacks (pages 62–64) get them through the drive home, but another round of eating is necessary as they walk in the door to fully regenerate from the school day. I find that the earlier we can get dinner on the table, the better. But in the meantime, a ready snack on the table is the most effective means to keep the peace, and a plate of homemade graham crackers with cream cheese or peanut butter saves us all from a tantrum or two in the hours to come.

For the best s'mores, put two of these beauties together with a Marshmallow (page 274) and a little brick of chocolate. Or reduce the crackers to crumbs for a Graham Cracker Crust (page 152).

GRAHAM CRACKERS   MAKES 45 TO 50 2 × 3-INCH CRACKERS

- 1 cup (5 ounces) all-purpose flour
- ¾ cup (3.38 ounces) whole wheat flour
- ½ cup (1.75 ounces) rye flour, plus more for dusting
- ½ teaspoon salt
- ¼ teaspoon baking soda
- ½ teaspoon baking powder
- 1½ teaspoons ground cinnamon
- ¼ cup (2 ounces) packed dark brown sugar, homemade (page 51) or store-bought
- 3 tablespoons cold unsalted butter, cut into 1-inch cubes
- 4 tablespoons (2 ounces) shortening (see page 217), cut into 1-inch cubes
- 4 tablespoons honey
- 2 teaspoons Vanilla Extract, homemade (page 65) or store-bought
- 1 teaspoon granulated sugar

storage

ROOM TEMPERATURE • covered container, 10 days

FRIDGE • unbaked dough in waxed paper, 3 days

FREEZER • unbaked dough, wrapped in plastic and a freezer bag, 4 months (thaw in the refrigerator before rolling out); baked crackers, freezer bag (recrisp in a 375°F oven for 5 minutes), 4 months

1   In the bowl of a stand mixer, combine the flours with the salt, baking soda, baking powder, 1 teaspoon of the cinnamon, and the brown sugar. Mix for 10 seconds using the paddle attachment, then add the butter and shortening. Mix on medium speed for 30 seconds.

2   Combine the honey and vanilla with ¼ cup cold water in a liquid measuring cup and stir to combine until the honey is mostly dissolved. With the mixer running on medium-low speed, slowly pour the honey mixture into the bowl, giving the mixture time to absorb the liquid. Continue to mix for another 20 seconds, or until the dough comes together. It will still be slightly crumbly. Push the dough into a ball, wrap it in waxed paper, and refrigerate for at least 2 hours, and up to 3 days. (The dough can be wrapped and frozen at this point.)

3   Take the dough out of the refrigerator about 20 minutes before you are ready to bake. Preheat the oven to 350°F. Cut the dough in half, and lay one half between two sheets of waxed paper dusted with rye flour. Roll the dough as thin as you can get it, ideally ⅛ inch. It will still be slightly crumbly, but just press it back together and keep rolling. Use a pizza wheel, crinkle cutter, or knife to cut 2 × 3-inch rectangles. Use a spatula to separate the rectangles from the waxed paper and set them on an ungreased baking sheet. The crackers won't spread, so they can be quite close. Reroll any scraps and repeat—then repeat again with the second half of the dough.

4   In a small bowl, combine the remaining ½ teaspoon cinnamon with the granulated sugar. Sprinkle the crackers with the cinnamon mixture and prick the dough several times with a fork. Bake for 15 minutes, or until just starting to brown at the edges. Cool on a wire rack. The crackers are great out of the oven, but their flavor and texture improves the next day.

BREAD-CRUMBS

—or—

cooking together

mY FRIEND SARAH and I are a pair of dragons in the kitchen. We're all power and fire, wrapping our necks around every dish and pan, alternating between high fives and biting comments.

Our mothers bonded in the early '80s over brown rice and adzuki beans. Both single parents, they recognized each other as sisters and decided to co-parent for a while. They sang in a New Age music band, and they dressed in purple silks and danced to the Jethro Tull–like flute. This left us free to wander—at two and three years old, we would make our way toward the woods behind the little house we all shared; stripped naked we would spread ourselves with the milk from the milkweed pods and call it suntan lotion. Our moms cooked for "opening the heart" workshops to pay the bills, and they still beam with pride when they talk about the weekend they made 10,000 tofu meatballs. They fought over men and solos in the band, and I'm guessing that those two were a pair of dragons in the kitchen, too.

Miraculously our mothers' friendship survived it all, and so has ours. Sarah and I rebelled against the whole grains from our childhood, and our cooking style is remarkably similar. When she visits or I am in her kitchen in Maine, we always end up wanting the same thing for dinner, yet our cooking methods are inevitably different. The result is that I walk out of these meals with new twists on my old meals—rutabaga in my shepherd's pie or garlic breadcrumbs on my mac and cheese.

Before I made macaroni and cheese with Sarah a few years ago, I had never made a breadcrumb in my life. Sarah had bought a cheap Italian loaf of bread at the supermarket and brushed every slice of it with garlic butter. It went into the oven, then into the Cuisinart, then onto the mac and cheese. I haven't bought another canister of breadcrumbs since then.

BREADCRUMBS MAKES 6 CUPS

1 Preheat the oven to 350°F.

2 Push the bread through the food processor's grater disc to create crumbs. Lay the breadcrumbs on a baking sheet (it's okay if they overlap) and bake for 20 to 30 minutes, or until just beginning to brown. Check on the breadcrumbs every 10 minutes, shuffling them around and checking on their texture. If you would like finer breadcrumbs, return them to the food processor after baking and chop with the chopping blade. Allow to cool before storing.

- 1 pound sliced White Bread, homemade (page 214) or store-bought, or about 15 slices

storage

FRIDGE · covered container or bag, 1 week

FREEZER · freezer-safe container or bag, 6 months (use directly from the freezer)

variations ~ GARLIC BREADCRUMBS (Especially wonderful on baked Macaroni and Cheese, page 200) Melt ½ stick unsalted butter together with 4 minced garlic cloves and ½ teaspoon salt. Spread the garlic butter on the bread before pressing through the food processor. QUICK BREADCRUMBS If you need a smaller amount of breadcrumbs in a shorter amount of time, make toast, then chop it in the food processor using the chopping blade.

f

OR A FEW YEARS I WORKED at Fabio's Seafood, a medium-class establishment that served shellfish in the landlocked mountains of Santa Fe. If you never had the fortune to dine there before they closed their doors, I'm sure that you have eaten at similar restaurants: polyester white linens, Andrea Bocelli on repeat, and surprisingly fantastic tomato sauce that makes the mural of Venice crudely spray-painted on the wall just tolerable. There are always breadsticks in a glass on the table when you sit down, and they are always addictive. I used to stand in the kitchen at Fabio's waiting for my customers to decide between the *spaghetti al vongole* and the *lobster a la Fabio,* all the while eating off the tray of breadsticks. I never had to eat the fish there—the breadsticks kept me going all night.

This recipe re-creates the Fabio's breadsticks as they stand in my memory. It comes from the book *Better than Store-Bought* (Harper and Row, 1979), a home-cooking manual after my own heart published in the late '70s. Pull the breadsticks as thin as you can get them—shoved into a glass onto your dinner table, they'll keep you fed through the evening, too. Or keep them shorter so you can fit them into lunch boxes. Although a breadstick is really just a glorified cracker, it's so much more fun to eat.

BREADSTICKS

MAKES THIRTY-TWO 8-INCH BREADSTICKS

- ½ teaspoon sugar
- 2 teaspoons active dry yeast
- ⅔ cup warm water (between 100°F and 110°F)
- 2 cups (10 ounces) all-purpose flour, plus additional for the counter
- 1½ teaspoons salt
- 2 tablespoons olive oil, plus additional for greasing the bowl and the baking sheets
- 2 tablespoons poppy or caraway seeds

1 Combine the sugar and yeast with the warm water in the bowl of a stand mixer, and let sit for 5 minutes. It should be slightly foamy. Add 1¼ cups of the flour and the salt and olive oil. Mix for 5 minutes on medium speed using the paddle attachment.

2 Dust the counter with the remaining ¾ cup flour. Turn the dough out onto the counter and knead the additional flour into the dough for 3 to 4 minutes, or until the dough is smooth and has lost most of its stickiness. Put the dough into a greased bowl, cover with plastic wrap, and allow it to rise until doubled in size. This will take 1 to 2 hours depending on the temperature in your kitchen.

3 Punch the air out of the dough with one swift punch, and turn the dough out on a floured counter again. Sprinkle the seeds onto the dough; then knead them into the dough for about 1 minute. Cover the dough with plastic and let rest for 5 minutes.

4 Remove the plastic wrap and set it aside. Divide the dough in half, then halves again, and then halves again. Repeat until you have 32 roughly equal pieces. Lay the plastic wrap over the balls of dough and set up your baking sheets, lined with parchment paper. Take each ball of dough, one at a time, and roll it between your hands until you have a breadstick that is about 8 inches long and no more than ½ inch in diameter. Lay the breadsticks on the tray with 2 inches between them. Let rest uncovered for 30 minutes. Meanwhile, preheat the oven to 325°F.

5 Bake the breadsticks for 35 to 40 minutes, or until they are slightly golden. Let cool entirely before storing.

storage

ROOM TEMPERATURE • covered container, 7 days

FREEZER • freezer-safe container or bag, 3 months (recrisp in a 375°F oven for 5 minutes)

m Y FRIEND MOLLY is always moving to a new country to save the world.

When someone compliments Sadie on her little doll with perfect shoes, she informs them that it was sewn by deaf orphans in Afghanistan, and that her auntie Molly helped the orphans get the fabric. As long as the girls have been alive, Molly has come home with beat-up suitcases filled with treasures.

As much as I desire to expose my girls to the world outside our tiny bubble, the cost of four plane tickets is prohibitive, and the girls seem to be most content within the parameters of the yard. So for now, we travel together through Auntie Molly, cooking with the spices she brings back, inhaling the woody scent of the rugs she rolls into her duffel bags, and nursing her through her jet lag and culture shock.

In exchange for the treasures that come home, I send cracker supplies to Molly. She is allergic to nearly everything, and so she begs for gluten-free pancake mix, millet, and rice flour. Out of desperation for a snack that she can eat, Molly has worked for years experimenting with flours and grains to create just the right crunch. She has skillfully re-created the wheat thin, and she makes a gluten-free version for herself on one tray, and a wheat version on the other for her husband. That wheat version has become my favorite cracker, and every time they come out of the oven, the girls are happy to know they are Molly's very own, even though we are separated by thousands of miles. Like the other treasures that Molly brings us, the girls prefer them to what we find at home.

"Mom, will you make real crackers this week?" Sadie asks. She adds, "You know, with a rolling pin."

And with that, the boxed crackers became the imitation, and I have found a way to satisfy all our cracker needs. Sadie and Joey are wheat-thin folks, but Rosie requires a steady diet of buttery cheese crackers.

WHEAT CRACKERS   MAKES 50 TO 60 CRACKERS

- 1 cup (5 ounces) all-purpose flour, plus additional for the counter
- 1 cup (4.75 ounces) spelt flour or whole wheat flour (4.5 ounces)
- ½ teaspoon baking powder
- ⅓ cup whole, uncooked millet
- ⅓ cup ground flax seeds
- ½ teaspoon kosher salt, plus additional for sprinkling
- *Optional:* 5 medium garlic cloves, minced, and 1 tablespoon minced fresh rosemary
- ½ cup plus 2 tablespoons olive oil
- Freshly ground pepper

1 Preheat the oven to 350°F. In a medium bowl, combine the two flours, baking powder, millet, flax, salt, and garlic and rosemary, if using. Add the olive oil and combine with a fork. Slowly add ½ cup water, mixing with your hands as you go. Continue to add more water (up to ¼ cup additional water) to the dough until it holds together. Knead the dough with your hands in the bowl for 2 minutes until it is smooth and very workable.

2 Turn out the dough onto a floured surface, press into a flat disc, and roll with a rolling pin until the dough is ⅛ to ¼ inch thick. For square crackers, use a pizza wheel or sharp knife and cut the dough into 2-inch squares. For round crackers, use a 2-inch biscuit cutter. Any leftover dough can be rerolled for more crackers.

3 With a spatula, transfer the cut dough to ungreased baking sheets and sprinkle each cracker with salt and pepper. Bake for 20 to 22 minutes, switching the position of the sheets and rotating them midway through, until the crackers are hard to the touch. Transfer to a wire rack.

storage

ROOM TEMPERATURE • covered container, 7 days

FREEZER • freezer-safe container or bag, 3 months (recrisp in a 375°F oven for 3 minutes)

variation ~ Make your crackers gluten-free! Substitute 1 cup each of brown rice flour and white rice flour for the wheat and spelt flours. Use an additional ¼ teaspoon baking powder and brush the dough with a little olive oil to make the salt and pepper stick. The dough is a little tougher to work with, but Molly advises you to "take your time! Flour every surface, and don't get too attached to perfectly square crackers."

CHEESE CRACKERS MAKES 40 TO 45 CRACKERS

1 Combine the butter, flour, dry mustard, and salt in the bowl of a stand mixer. Mix on low speed with the paddle attachment until the mixture is crumbly and the butter starts to integrate into the mixture, about 30 seconds. Add the cheese and mix again on low speed for a few seconds.

2 In a liquid measuring cup, combine ¾ cup water, the vinegar, and the ice cube and let sit for a moment to get cold. Add 6 tablespoons of the vinegar mixture to the dough and mix on medium speed for 20 seconds. Continue to add liquid, 1 tablespoon at a time, until the dough clings in a ball to the beater. Then mix for an additional 30 seconds. Mound the dough into a ball, wrap it in waxed paper or plastic wrap, and refrigerate for at least 2 hours, and up to 3 days.

3 Remove the dough from the refrigerator 15 minutes before you are ready to roll it out. Preheat the oven to 325°F and grease two baking sheets. Turn out the dough onto a floured surface, press into a flat disc, and roll with a rolling pin until the dough is ⅛ to ¼ inch thick. For square crackers, use a pizza wheel or sharp knife and cut the dough into 2-inch squares. For round crackers, use a 2-inch biscuit cutter. Any leftover dough can be rerolled for more crackers.

4 With a spatula, transfer crackers to greased baking sheets, allowing 1 inch between crackers. Bake for 30 minutes, rotating the trays halfway through baking, or until the crackers are slightly golden. Turn off the oven, but leave the trays in the oven as it cools for at least 1 hour.

storage
ROOM TEMPERATURE • covered container, 5 to 7 days
FRIDGE • unbaked dough, wrapped in plastic wrap, 3 days
FREEZER • unbaked dough, wrapped in plastic and a freezer bag, 4 months (thaw in refrigerator before rolling out); baked crackers, freezer bag, 4 months (recrisp in a 375°F oven for 5 minutes)

- 3 tablespoons unsalted cold butter, cut into 1-inch cubes, plus additional for the baking sheets
- 1½ cups (7.5 ounces) all-purpose flour, plus additional for the counter
- 1 teaspoon dry mustard powder
- 1 teaspoon salt
- 1½ cups (6 ounces) grated Cheddar cheese
- 2 teaspoons distilled white vinegar
- 1 ice cube

10
drinks

lemonade

chai

tea
my favorite tea
lavender
chamomile tea
rose scented tea

soda
rhubarb ginger syrup
herb syrup
berry syrup

hot chocolate

liqueurs
coffee liqueur

amaretto

LEMONADE
—or—
work, passion, and money

i CANNOT FIGURE OUT the relationship between work and money. Everyone comes at it differently, and I drink in all the advice I get.

"Do what you love for free, then get a job." This goes with the rationale that money corrupts one's love of a thing, so I say yes! I will write for free and wait tables for rent. Then there is, "Do what you love, and the money comes." This is also true, and it's lovely to think that if you just stick to your passion, the details take care of themselves.

I have always felt fortunate that I needed to work, and from my first job when I was fourteen, I have supported my needs in some way with my paycheck. And although I try not to complicate the girls' lives with too much knowledge of our financial affairs, there has to be some reason there is not a constant stream of American Girl doll clothes and why we abstain from the school book order in favor of the library. I empty my pockets of change to pay for a hot chocolate on a special occasion Tuesday.

"Why don't you go to the ATM, Mom? They always have money for you there."

It's a confusing world we live in. And to combat the claims of "we don't have money for that," Sadie has begun to express her entrepreneurial soul, whether planning a tag sale or creating a business to water the neighbors' plants. Nothing quite makes it out of the imagination stage, and few ideas reach the excitement of the classic lemonade stand.

In the girls' eyes, Daddy is a teacher because he is a great teacher, and Mommy writes and cooks because she's a little crazy when she doesn't. I'll keep trying to figure it out for myself in the hopes of being a model for them. In the meantime, Sadie practices her lemonade skills, and one of these days she's going to have one hell of a lemonade stand.

LEMONADE   MAKES 8 CUPS

- ½ cup sugar or honey
- 7 cups water
- ¾ cup fresh lemon juice (from 4 to 5 lemons)

1 Combine the sugar and 1 cup of water in a small saucepan. Heat over medium-low heat until the sugar is dissolved.

2 Combine the sugar water, lemon juice, and remaining 6 cups of water in a pitcher. Use a long-handled spoon to stir to combine. Chill in the refrigerator or pour over ice.

storage

FRIDGE · covered container, 5 days

FREEZER · freezer-safe container, 6 months (thaw in refrigerator)

i LOVE TO BE SOMEWHERE ELSE. I love to get the words of other languages stuck in my head like a song, to get lost and know that I might need charades to find my way back. I love to brush by people on the street or the bus who are so different from me and have never been to where I am from. They're also trying to pick up their kids from school on time; they need to stop by the market and grab something for dinner. When I travel, I always come home with every cell in my body humming.

The strong black tea of Istanbul comes in a little tulip-shaped glass with a bowl of sugar cubes on the side. It is always time for a cup of tea in Istanbul, and after ten minutes of pushing our way through a busy street smelling of cats and saffron, my friend Lissa and I would look at each other with the contented look of friends who are thinking the same thing, and within moments, we would be at a wicker table on the street, holding up two fingers to order "*iki tani* (two) *cay* (teas)." Trying to bring Istanbul home with me, I carefully packed a tiny glass teacup in my suitcase, and I swore to Lissa that I would have tea in this glass in my own kitchen.

One day, after visiting the Blue Mosque and the Hagia Sofia, we rested in a park perched between the two buildings. At 4:00 P.M., men arrived with carafes of sweet spiced tea. The air became a fog of cinnamon and cloves, and I imagined those golden thermoses to be filled with spicy milky ambrosia. We watched the men maneuver the great vats around the park benches, dispensing tea into small paper cups with a tube affixed to the container. I later learned that the heavenly steam was coming from *salep,* a tea made with orchid roots(!), milk, and spices. I am ashamed that I held back and didn't try it, and I promise to become a better traveler. I will get better at learning difficult words, and I will ask for whatever the locals are drinking.

This is the spiced tea of my own kitchen. I drink it in my Turkish cup, and the air around me feels just different enough.

CHAI MAKES 6 CUPS

1 Combine the water, ginger, cinnamon, cloves, cardamom, peppercorns, and orange slice in a medium pot. Partially cover the pot, bring the mixture to a boil, reduce the heat, and simmer for 15 minutes.

2 Take the pot off the heat, add the tea bags, cover, and steep for 5 minutes. Put a strainer over a bowl and strain the liquid. Add the honey to taste. To store the chai in the refrigerator or freezer without milk, do so now. Otherwise, return the tea to the pot, add the milk, and reheat.

storage

FRIDGE • covered container, with milk, 5 days; without milk, 2 weeks

FREEZER • freezer-safe container, without milk, 6 months (thaw in refrigerator and reheat with milk on the stovetop)

- 5 cups water
- ¼ cup roughly chopped unpeeled fresh ginger
- Three 4-inch cinnamon sticks
- 3 whole cloves
- 4 cardamom pods
- 3 black peppercorns
- One 1-inch circular slice unpeeled orange
- 4 black tea bags, regular or decaffeinated
- ¼ to ½ cup honey, to taste
- 1½ to 2 cups milk (low-fat or whole), to taste

i FOUND MY FAVORITE TEA BLEND, and then I lost it. It was made by an obscure tea company, and I regularly shelled out four bucks a box for that very herbal combination. It was fruity, tart, and minty all at once—good for sickness, wellness, or iced tea. I seemed to be the only one who liked it, because one day it was gone from the shelves, and I learned that the blend had been discontinued.

One day my friend Jen was in the kitchen, and I set the kettle on the stove. She is an herbalist and a farmer, and she perused my meager and mostly caffeinated tea drawer.

"They don't make my tea anymore," I started my tea rant. "You'll just have to have chamomile."

For someone who makes so many basic foods at home, it doesn't always occur to me to do so. Jen let out a good laugh before reminding me that we could actually put my tea blend together ourselves. It would, of course, stay fresher and taste better and cost less than a box of tea bags.

I found my tea once again, and then I found a few others. Now I have jars on my shelf of my very own tea mixes. Many are even made from herbs I have grown, and you can grow herbs or buy in bulk to make your own, too. Most herbs will dry well in a warm and shady spot laid out on a screen for ten days, and herbs with higher moisture content like mint and lemon balm will dry in a dehydrator. Enjoy your perfect tea.

TEAS

MY FAVORITE TEA

- 1 cup dried hibiscus flowers
- 2 tablespoons dried rosehips
- ½ cup dried spearmint leaves

LAVENDER CHAMOMILE

- ¾ cup dried lavender flowers
- 1 cup dried chamomile stems and flowers
- 1 tablespoon dried spearmint leaves

ROSE-SCENTED TEA

- 1½ cups loose black tea
- ¼ cup dried rose petals
- 1 tablespoon cardamom seeds (crush green cardamom pods in a mortar and pestle to release the seeds inside)

1 Combine the ingredients in a 2-cup jar and seal with the lid. Shake gently to combine.

2 To brew a cup of tea, boil water in a kettle or pot. Put a tablespoon of tea into a tea ball or tea strainer, and pour the boiling water over the tea. Steep for 5 minutes, sweeten with sugar or honey if you like, and serve.

storage

ROOM TEMPERATURE • airtight jar, 1 year

nO MATTER WHAT we may tell our children about the evils of soda, there is nothing so thirst-quenching as a glass of something sweet and carbonated.

When I was a child, my grandparents would take me out to dinner, and they would give in to my ginger ale begging, and without fail I would be stuffed with sweet bubbles before dinner arrived. So on our occasional family nights out, it's water for the ladies. They have come to accept soda as a treat to be consumed on its own like ice cream or candy so it can be appreciated in all its deliciousness.

I have a weakness for soda. Joey gets a Coke whenever we go out. I drain half the glass when his back is turned. It was my friend Janet who taught me about fruit syrups and seltzer (a far superior creation to the juice and seltzer "jeltzer" that my children abhor).

One hot spring day, I found myself canceling an anticipated tea date with Janet. I left her a quick message, "Can't meet. Must type. Under deadline." An hour later, the kitchen door opened and Janet snuck in carrying a lovely pink bottle in one hand and a bottle of bubbly water in the other.

"I'm not here," she said, digging around in my freezer for ice. She grabbed a glass, poured some of each bottle into it, and held it out to me.

If summer came in a glass, it would be pink and full of bubbles, spicy with ginger and cool with lime. I drank the whole glass, and then I had another. As soon as I had Janet's recipe, there was no end to the possibilities. Herbs, berries, anything was fair game when combined with a little sugar, and we had the most exotic and wonderful sodas.

These syrups can be used according to your preference. Two tablespoons make a flavored seltzer, and $1/3$ cup syrup in 1 cup of seltzer makes a full-blown soda. Serve chilled or over ice according to your taste. And mixed with vodka or gin, it's fancy cocktail hour at your house.

RHUBARB GINGER SYRUP   MAKES 6 TO 7 CUPS

1 Combine the rhubarb and water in a medium saucepan and bring to a boil over medium-high heat. Reduce the heat to low, and cook for about 20 minutes, or until the rhubarb is almost dissolving. Use a slotted spoon to scoop out the rhubarb (see Note, page 246).

2 Add the lime juice to the rhubarb water, along with the ginger and sugar. Raise the heat to medium-high and cook at a low boil, uncovered, for 20 minutes, or until the mixture is slightly reduced and thickened.

3 Remove it from the heat, add your herb of choice, and cover. Let steep for 5 to 10 minutes. Taste and add sugar if needed. Strain through a fine-meshed sieve into a jar or bottle and let cool.

- 2 pounds rhubarb, cut into 1-inch pieces
- 8 cups water
- 4 tablespoons fresh lime juice (from 2 to 3 limes)
- 1 tablespoon fresh ginger, peeled and roughly chopped
- ½ cup sugar or more to taste
- A few sprigs of fresh thyme or a handful of fresh lemon balm, mint, or a combination of the two

HERB SYRUP   MAKES 2 CUPS

- 4 ounces fresh mint, basil, lemon verbena, or lemon balm leaves (or a combination), roughly chopped
- 2 tablespoons fresh lemon juice (from 1 lemon)
- 1½ cups sugar
- 2 cups water

1 Combine the chopped herbs and the lemon juice with 1 tablespoon of the sugar in a small bowl. Mash these ingredients with a spoon or your fingers and set aside.

2 Bring the water to a boil in a medium saucepan, then remove from the heat. Stir in the remaining sugar and continue to stir until the sugar is dissolved. Add the herb mixture to the saucepan, cover, and let sit undisturbed for 15 minutes. Pour the mixture through a fine-meshed sieve into a jar or bottle and let cool.

BERRY SYRUP   MAKES 5 TO 6 CUPS

- 2 pounds fresh or frozen berries (blackberries, raspberries, blueberries, strawberries, currants, or a combination)
- 6 cups water
- 3 tablespoons fresh lemon juice (from 1 to 2 lemons)
- ½ cup sugar or more to taste
- *Optional:* 1 tablespoon kirsch liqueur

note ~ Save the pulp, sweeten with sugar or honey, and serve over yogurt or ice cream.

1 Combine the berries and water in a large saucepan. Bring to a boil, reduce the heat, cover, and cook for at least 20 minutes, or until the berries are dissolved or mostly broken up.

2 Blend the mixture using an immersion blender or transfer to an upright blender. Pour the mixture through a sieve into a mixing bowl (see Note), then return to the pan and add the lemon juice and ½ cup sugar. Cook over medium-high heat at a very low boil for 15 minutes, stirring frequently, until slightly reduced. Add additional sugar to taste. Stir in the kirsch, if using, and allow to cool.

storage (all syrups)
FRIDGE • covered bottle or jar, 10 days
FREEZER • covered bottle or jar, 6 months

i GET MYSELF INTO TROUBLE with my constant need for efficiency and purpose. Joey comes home from work exhausted, grabs a *New Yorker*, and sits on the couch for a few minutes. He needs a break and he takes a break. I'm trying to learn the skill, but it's slow going.

As a practice in enjoyment for enjoyment's sake, I drink hot chocolate whenever I have the chance. All of the other hot drinks that people bustle around with have such a purpose. Tired? Grab a coffee, or if you've had too much coffee already, black tea. Sniffly? Herbal tea. Just want to have something wonderful in your cup? Hot chocolate, maybe even with whipped cream or marshmallows. It's a luxury drink, the beverage of princesses in bed who have nothing to do all day, the drink of children out for a treat. I skip the powder and go for the chunks of chocolate, melted into steamy milk like it never hoped to be eaten on its own.

How much chocolate you add here is up to your taste and the kind of chocolate you use—less chocolate will make a mellow hot chocolate that won't make kids bonkers, and more will make a thick and intense chocolate elixir.

HOT CHOCOLATE   MAKES 4 CUPS

- 4 cups whole milk
- 3 to 5 ounces sweetened chocolate (dark or milk), roughly chopped
- 1 teaspoon vanilla extract
- *Optional:* Whipped Cream (page 279); Marshmallows, homemade (page 274) or store-bought

Heat the milk over medium heat in a medium saucepan until it just starts to steam. Put the chocolate in the pan and whisk it until it is entirely melted and incorporated. Serve in a mug, hot, topped with whipped cream or marshmallows, if you like.

storage

FRIDGE • covered container, 3 days (reheat on the stove while whisking)

FREEZER • no

i'VE NEVER BEEN ABLE TO PULL OFF a drink order without cracking a smile, and I will always be a geek at the bar, no matter how old I get. I don't end up at bars often, but when I do, I spend the way to the bar thinking about what I'll order, so that when the cocktail waitress skids up to the table with impatience, I can exhale my drink order like it was the most natural thing in the world. Instead, I crack a smile, and it's like I'm sixteen and getting away with ordering a drink.

The white Russian is my secret weapon. I've been drinking them since before I came of age, but the Coen brothers made them hip back in the '90s and so I never lose face. There is always a surprised, "I love white Russians!" and usually someone follows my order by copying it, and then sneaks in some reference to "the dude" from *The Big Lebowski*.

On New Year's Eve, we fill up the house with everyone we know—our tradition is to draw a line on the floor and hop over it at 7:00. That hop takes us over to England, and we listen to British radio on the Internet so we can all celebrate the new year at a reasonable hour. All fall I think about what I'll feed the masses on New Year's Eve (chili, again?), and what cocktail I will hand to guests as they shake the snow out of their hair. Last year I made a big batch of coffee liqueur, and because that cost next to nothing I spent my booze money on local vodka to mix with the coffee liqueur. Combined with fresh milk from down the street, the liqueur makes the most fantastic white Russians, and I confirmed my suspicion that everyone does, indeed, love a white Russian.

Here are two recipes for simple homemade liqueurs. Make some for yourself and give the rest away. To give as a gift, pour coffee liqueur or amaretto into smaller bottles and put half a vanilla bean in each bottle.

COFFEE LIQUEUR MAKES 8 CUPS

- 4 cups water
- 2 cups sugar
- 4½ tablespoons instant coffee
- 4 cups cheap vodka
- 2 vanilla beans

I THANK RACHEL FLETCHER, who keeps all of Berkshire County in homemade liqueur, for inspiration on this recipe. I met Rachel's brew before I met Rachel—she says she gifts at least eighty bottles a year.

1   Combine the water, sugar, and instant coffee in a large saucepan and bring to a high simmer, but not a boil. Cover and cook for 1 hour, taking care that it continues to simmer without coming to a boil.

2   Let the mixture cool and add the vodka, stirring to combine. Transfer to a bottle or jar, add the vanilla beans, screw on the lid, and keep in a cool, dark place for at least 2 weeks before serving (though it will taste even better as time passes).

storage

ROOM TEMPERATURE • airtight bottle, 6 months
FREEZER • airtight bottle, 2 years

AMARETTO   MAKES 4 CUPS

HOMEMADE AMARETTO IS THINNER THAN STORE-BOUGHT, and less syrupy. Without all that thick sweetness, the almond flavor really shines through.

1   Combine the brown sugar with ½ cup of water in a small saucepan. Heat until the sugar is dissolved, then let cool.

2   Use a paring knife to split the vanilla bean from one end to the other to expose the sticky seeds inside.

3   Pour the liquid into a bottle or jar, then add the split vanilla bean, vodka, and almond extract. Top with the lid and shake to combine. The amaretto is ready to drink immediately, but will get better with age.

storage
ROOM TEMPERATURE • airtight bottle, 6 months
FREEZER • airtight bottle, 2 years

- 1 cup (8 ounces) packed light brown sugar, homemade (page 51) or store-bought
- 1 vanilla bean
- 3½ cups cheap vodka
- 4 tablespoons almond extract

CANDY
—or—
the holiday mash up

WHEN SADIE WAS THREE, she came home from school in December asking, "Who is Christ? Is Christmas really his birthday party?" These are the moments I wish we had a rabbi or a rector or a guru.

Technically we're Jews and I have a little Episcopalian in there, too. I grew up with latkes and matzoh balls served on pagan holidays by my goddess-worshipping, Yiddish-speaking grandmother. Joey is the son of New York Jews who worshipped the erotic part of the Old Testament and ate a lot of lox. Together we try to find the right answers to the questions, and we create our own rituals for the winter holidays.

Our holiday season begins with Thanksgiving. Then we light the candles of the menorah. *"Barukh atah Adonai, Eloheinu, melekh ha'olam,* mutter, mutter." The girls launch into, "Oh Hanukkah, come light the menorah!" Somewhere in there comes the solstice when we read Kazuo Iwamura's *The Winter Sledding Day* and eat pomegranates as we talk about Persephone and why there is winter. All the while, there is the soundtrack to *Charlie Brown Christmas.* And finally there is Christmas, and we walk outside all morning and come back to open one gift for each of us under the tree. Then we order Chinese food, and we finalize the menu for our annual New Year's party.

Although some would find our holiday mishmash sacrilegious, it feels like there is plenty of God and love and giving. At first the giving was all Joey, and he made mix CDs and hand-cut ornaments for our friends. Then my cookies and candies appeared next to his mix CDs in take-out boxes decorated by the girls. I started making the easiest (and now sought after) chocolates I could find. Since I was melting chocolate anyway, I figured I might as well make peanut butter cups, and then there were lavender caramels and fleur de sel caramels. I make candy only once a year and I am always struck by the ease of it. Then I forget and another year goes by before I make candy again.

EASIEST CHOCOLATES
MAKES 20 CHOCOLATES

- Canola oil, for greasing
- 1¼ pounds decent quality bittersweet chocolate, broken into large pieces
- 1⅓ cups dried fruit, roughly chopped
- 1⅓ cups nuts, roughly chopped
- Sea salt or fleur de sel

THIS RECIPE CAME TO ME with the help of Molly Wizenberg through her blog *Orangette*, and she got it from *Gourmet*. It's more of a method, and the possible combinations are endless. Some of my favorites are dried cranberries, crystallized ginger, and almonds; dried blueberries and pecans; and apricots and pistachios. If you are one of those who cannot abide chocolate and fruit combinations, feel free to go entirely off the map.

1 Set up your double boiler (see below), and grease a 9-inch square pan with oil. Melt the chocolate in the double boiler, stirring as it melts. When it is entirely smooth, remove it from the heat. Stir the fruit and nuts into the chocolate.

2 Pour the mixture into your prepared pan, and sprinkle the whole thing with salt. Cover lightly with a loose piece of plastic wrap or a towel and refrigerate for at least 4 hours.

3 Remove from the refrigerator, turn the chocolate out onto the counter, and use a sharp knife to cut into 20 rectangles.

storage
ROOM TEMPERATURE • covered container, 3 days (just long enough to send in the mail)
FRIDGE • covered container, 2 weeks
FREEZER • freezer-safe container, 3 months (eat directly from the freezer or thaw in the refrigerator)

---

the double boiler setup ~ Chocolate needs to melt without direct heat, so you can melt it in a double boiler. All you need is a saucepan and a metal or glass heatproof bowl. The bowl should fit snuggly into the rim of the saucepan, and the bottom of the bowl should be several inches from the bottom of the saucepan. Fill the saucepan with 1 to 2 inches of water and bring it to a simmer. Set the bowl over the saucepan and stir as the contents are warmed by the steam from the water in the saucepan.

PEANUT BUTTER CUPS

WHILE THESE TAKE SOME TIME to set up and fill, they're fabulous and have a nice bit of goosh to them. You can also take a few extra minutes to make your peanut butter from scratch. This is a moment when it really shines.

- 1 pound bittersweet chocolate or milk chocolate, roughly chopped
- 1 cup creamy or chunky peanut butter, homemade (page 121) or store-bought
- ½ teaspoon Vanilla Extract, homemade (page 165) or store-bought
- ¼ teaspoon salt
- 2 tablespoons packed light brown sugar, homemade (page 51) or store-bought

1 Lay out 30 mini muffin liners (petits-fours papers) on a large plate or baking sheet. Set up a double boiler (see page 258) over medium heat. Melt the chocolate in the double boiler, stirring it as it melts, and when it is entirely smooth, 7 to 10 minutes, remove it from the heat.

2 Scoop up a bit of chocolate with a small spoon, pour it into a mini muffin liner, and use the back of the spoon to spread the chocolate around the entire inside of the liner. You want the layer of chocolate to be thin, but not so thin that it won't hold up when it dries and gets peeled out of the paper. Repeat with the remaining cups. Set them aside to harden a bit, 10 to 15 minutes, and wash the spoon. Set aside the remaining melted chocolate.

3 Meanwhile, make the filling. Combine the peanut butter, vanilla, salt, and brown sugar in the bowl of a food processor fitted with the chopping blade. Process the mixture until it is smooth and uniform.

4 Even if the chocolate is not yet hard, with the small spoon, fill each cup three-fourths of the way with the peanut butter mixture.

5 Return the double boiler to medium heat, and soften the remaining chocolate in the bowl. With a large spoon, cover the peanut butter with melted chocolate to the top of the cups to seal in the filling. When all of the cups are filled, leave them to harden at room temperature for at least 3 hours.

storage
ROOM TEMPERATURE • covered container, 2 weeks
FRIDGE • covered container, 1 month
FREEZER • freezer-safe container or bag, 3 months

CARAMELS MAKES 65 TO 75 CANDIES

- Canola oil or baking spray
- 1 cup sugar
- 1 cup Lyle's Golden Syrup (see page 63)
- ½ teaspoon kosher salt
- 2 cups heavy cream
- 4 tablespoons (½ stick) unsalted butter, at room temperature, cut into chunks
- 1 teaspoon Vanilla Extract, homemade (page 165) or store-bought

YOU CAN MAKE CARAMELS to whatever texture and intensity that suits you. I like a soft and mild caramel, so that is what we are making here. Thanks to Alice Medrich (*Pure Dessert*, Artisan, 2007) for the suggestion to use Golden Syrup in the caramels. It creates the perfect buttery sweetness.

1   Line a 9-inch square baking pan with enough aluminum foil so that the foil hangs over the sides of the pan, then lightly grease the foil. Fill a small bowl with cold water, put a pastry brush in the water, and set it on your work surface.

2   Combine the sugar, syrup, and salt in a medium saucepan over medium heat, stirring with a wooden spoon to combine. When the mixture begins to bubble around the edges, use the wet pastry brush to brush the sugar crystals off the sides of the pan. Affix a candy thermometer to the side of the pan so that it is not touching the bottom. From this point on, no stirring! Cook the caramel without stirring until it reaches 238°F and is a medium amber color. Remove from heat (it will reach 240°F as you pull it off the heat).

3   Meanwhile, pour the cream into a small saucepan over medium-low heat and bring to a low simmer. Remove from heat, cover, and set aside.

4   Add the softened butter and warm cream to the caramel, stirring with the wooden spoon to combine. It will bubble and spurt, so stir until it calms down. Place the pot of caramel back over medium heat and bring it back up to 238°F, stirring frequently, 15 to 20 minutes.

5   Remove the caramel from the heat. Use a wooden spoon to stir in the vanilla (once again it will sputter!). Pour the mixture into the prepared pan. Set the pan aside and let sit undisturbed for at least 5 hours.

6 Pull out the whole square of caramel using the foil peeking out over the sides of the pan, lay it on a cutting board, and remove the foil. The caramel will be firm enough to hold its shape, but not firm enough to cut with a knife. Grab about 1 teaspoon of it with your hands and roll into a ball. Wrap in a small square of parchment, shaping it into a cylinder and twisting the ends to seal. Repeat with remaining caramel.

storage

ROOM TEMPERATURE • wrapped candies, 3 weeks
FREEZER • wrapped candies in a freezer bag, 3 months (thaw at room temperature)

tense moments ~ While caramels are not so hard to make, caramel wrapping is an entirely different story. Nothing kills the thrill of candy making like being trapped in the kitchen with a mountain of caramel and a roll of parchment paper after your family has long gone to sleep. To avoid too many tense moments, this is a project that Joey and I take on together, and we've finally learned to make a night of it. First, we cut the parchment squares; then I separate and shape the caramels while Joey wraps them. It may take as much as an hour to wrap the caramels, so pick out a good movie or podcast to pass the time.

variations ~ All sorts of flavorings are possible! Steep ½ cup dried lavender flowers or 1 teaspoon ground cardamom in the hot cream for 15 minutes, then strain before adding cream to the caramel. For fleur de sel caramels, sprinkle the greased foil with fleur de sel, then sprinkle it again on top of the caramel after you have poured it into the pan.

If you would like your caramels to be more like hard candies, bring the sugar mixture up to 260°F before you remove it from heat in step 4. Instead of shaping them with your hands before wrapping, cut with a greased knife.

FRUIT ROLLUPS

—or—

the cycle

WHEN I WAS YOUNG, I swore that I would never feed my children fruit leathers. Perhaps you know the ones I'm taking about—those geeky cousins to the fruit rollup, thick and sweetened with apple juice that most importantly *do not roll up.* While I was gnawing those hard and rubbery strips of dehydrated fruit product, the rest of the lunch table was eating fruit rollups. Ruby red, rolled like an unopened toy—those flawless sheets of sticky sweetness glistened in the sun of the cafeteria as they emerged from every other lunchbox but mine.

What once seemed to be my mother's simple denial of all things delicious and normal is now clear to me smart thinking on her part. I look at the long list of unpronounceable ingredients on the side of that box that they are begging for, and like my mother, although I would love to ease the pain they feel with the lack of that desired treat, I just can't bring myself to throw the box in the cart. I get it, Mom. I really do. I'm sorry it took me so long to understand.

My girls don't go for the "fruit leathers," either. The key to making the real deal are the two things that were missing from those leathers of my childhood: sweetness and rollability. I've found that the thinner the better, and a good bit of honey sweetens them just enough.

One of the great aspects of making food at home is that you are not bound to someone else's boring flavor combinations. Blackberry-rhubarb and strawberry-peach are two of my favorites, but feel free to create new flavors with every batch.

FRUIT ROLLUPS   MAKES 2 TO 3 DEHYDRATOR TRAYS OR 2 BAKING SHEETS

- 3 pounds fresh or frozen fruit (berries can be whole, apples quartered but not cored or peeled, mangoes peeled and pitted, any stone fruit pitted, rhubarb cut into 2-inch chunks)
- 2 tablespoons fresh lemon juice (from 1 lemon)
- ½ cup honey, or more to taste
- 1 cup Applesauce, homemade (page 81) or store-bought

1 Combine the fruit and lemon juice in a medium saucepan over medium heat. Cook, stirring occasionally, for about 20 minutes or until the fruit is entirely softened. Pass the puree through a food mill or fine-meshed sieve. Add the honey and applesauce and stir thoroughly. Taste and adjust the honey to your desired sweetness.

2 *If using a dehydrator,* follow the directions provided with your machine. Make sure that you pour the puree as thin as possible, and that you dehydrate the sheets until they are mostly dry to the touch with just a bit of stickiness. This will take between 12 and 20 hours, depending on your mixture. *If using an oven,* line two baking sheets with parchment. Pour the puree onto the baking sheets and bake at the lowest possible temperature for your oven (165°F is ideal) for 12 to 20 hours, or until dry to the touch with just a bit of stickiness.

3 Lay the finished sheets over parchment, and with scissors, cut both layers together in rectangles. Roll the fruit and parchment together in small rolls.

storage
ROOM TEMPERATURE • covered container, 1 month
FRIDGE • covered container, 2 months
FREEZER • freezer bag, 6 months (thaw at room temperature)

---

tense moments ~ The drying of your fruit rollup will vary with your equipment and the fruit that you use, so go by feel instead of the time that you expect. I once forgot all about my fruit rollups and by the time I got to them, they were fruit chips. If this happens to you, just change the name of the snack! Fruit chips went over pretty well at my house.

i LEARNED HOW TO BAKE the summer that Joey and I lived in a yurt in New Mexico. I worked at Counter Culture Cafe, where you can sit and drink coffee while you write or you can bring your parents for a great meal.

Bundt was the chosen cake shape on the counter and there were chocolate and sour cream coffee cake varieties. The muffins, usually blueberry, were almost all top. On the weekends, there were cinnamon rolls to make you sing. In May, the husband-and-wife owners, Jason and Elaine, hired me for the counter, and by June I started working earlier in the day in the kitchen, humming to myself alone while I whisked and stirred and melted.

Joey and I subletted the yurt outside of town for fifty dollars a month, and by 7:00 A.M. it was an oven in there. We'd get out just as the sun was rising and Joey would drop me off and head to his job down the street. I loved those mornings, and every week, Elaine would pop in during my shift and teach me a new skill. We'd chat while the mixer mixed, and in every conversation she'd find a way to slip in her most pressing piece of advice.

"Don't get pregnant."

By August, I had outgrown my jeans and Joey and I were planning our migration to New England to prepare for parenthood. But that summer's baking education came east with me, and with it, the joy and simplicity of cake, in both its creation and its consumption. Whether in a muffin or a birthday cake, the coming together of flour and butter and sugar and eggs will, with a little leavening, make cake that will almost always be good.

Thirty-seven ingredients are melded together to form America's most beloved cake, the Twinkie. The complexity of the cream-filled snack cake has inspired awe and books and art projects. I keep these cakes simple, and although they may not have the shelf life of these other ones, Joey assures me that they pass the test.

THE CREAM-FILLED SNACK CAKE   MAKES 12 CAKES

1 **MAKE THE CAKES.** Make a mold that is the shape of half of a 3- to 4-inch-wide spice jar. Rip aluminum foil into strips that are about 4 × 12 inches. Fold each piece in half so you have a double layer. Shape the foil around the spice jar and tuck it in the sides so that you have a half-cylinder mold that is as smooth as possible on the inside. Set it into a 9 × 13-inch baking dish and repeat until you have 12 little boat-shaped molds. Spray the inside of the molds with cooking spray. Preheat the oven to 350°F.

2 Combine the flour, baking powder, and salt in a mixing bowl and stir until thoroughly combined. Put the egg whites in the bowl of a stand mixer and beat with the wire whip attachment until the whites hold soft peaks. Gently transfer the beaten whites to another bowl and set aside. Rinse the mixer bowl and dry it thoroughly.

3 Put the butter in the mixer bowl and beat with the paddle until the butter starts to get light and fluffy, about 1 minute. Add the sugar and beat again until fluffy, about 2 more minutes. Add the egg yolks and vanilla, and beat to combine.

4 Add a third of the flour mixture to the mixer bowl, beat for a moment, then add half the milk and beat for a moment. Add one more third of the flour, beat, then the rest of the milk, then the rest of the flour. Make sure that the flour and milk are entirely incorporated. Then stir a third of the beaten egg whites into the batter. When that is fully incorporated, gently fold in the rest of the beaten egg whites.

5 Use a pastry bag to pipe the batter into the prepared molds, filling each one just under halfway. Bake for 25 to 30 minutes, or until the cakes start to turn golden and a cake tester or toothpick, when inserted, comes out clean. Allow the cakes to cool entirely.

recipe continues

FOR THE CAKES
- Cooking spray
- 1½ cups (6 ounces) sifted cake flour
- 2 teaspoons baking powder
- ¼ teaspoon salt
- 2 large eggs, separated
- ½ cup (1 stick) unsalted butter, at room temperature
- 1 cup granulated sugar
- 1 teaspoon Vanilla Extract, homemade (page 165) or store-bought
- ½ cup whole milk

FOR THE FILLING
- 4 tablespoons (2 ounces) nonhydrogenated vegetable shortening (see page 217), at room temperature
- 4 tablespoons (½ stick) unsalted butter, at room temperature
- ¼ teaspoon salt
- ½ cup powdered sugar
- 1 teaspoon Vanilla Extract, homemade (page 165) or store-bought

6   Unwrap the foil from each cake, and use a knife to make a 2- to 3-inch cut in the bottom. The cut should go about halfway into each cake. Wash the pastry bag and the mixer bowl.

7   **MAKE THE FILLING.** Combine the shortening, butter, salt, powdered sugar, and vanilla in the mixer bowl. Beat with the paddle attachment until fluffy, about 3 minutes.

8   Scoop the filling into a pastry bag and stick the tip into the cut at the bottom of each cake. Keep squeezing the pastry bag until the filling begins to leak out around the tip of the pastry bag. Then it's ready.

storage

ROOM TEMPERATURE • covered container, 3 days

FRIDGE • filling only, covered container, 10 days

FREEZER • cakes, wrapped in foil and a freezer bag, 3 months (thaw at room temperature); filling, freezer-safe container, 3 months (thaw in refrigerator)

---

tense moments ~ Making the molds for these little cakes is a project, and you will likely spend more time making the molds than making the batter. Don't skimp on the cooking spray and the cakes will come right out of the foil. Also, do your best to get the inside of each mold smooth—your cakes will be smoother.

The project requires a ridiculous amount of aluminum foil. In my kitchen, snack cakes are a once-in-a-while special treat, but if you are inspired to make them regularly, you can invest in a special pan called a canoe pan, which will do the same job as the aluminum foil.

---

m Y STEPFATHER, Chris, often passes through the kitchen with some purpose in mind, and inevitably he pauses in front of the pantry shelves, trying to be subtle as he hovers and searches for some container with the last bar or cookie that I've been concocting around here.

"Second shelf on the right. Behind that jar of flour."

He is an enthusiastic taste tester and has repeatedly remarked on a certain mysterious quality to the homemade treats that come out of my oven.

"They taste better. Always better! But still, I only want a few—and then I'm done." And with that, he has isolated the one element that I can't seem to re-create at home: the inexplicable and most likely unpronounceable ingredient that makes snack foods so addictive, so impossible to just eat the laughable serving size that is listed on the back of the package: two cookies? ten potato chips? four crackers? In one mouthful, maybe.

I'm guessing that we all have those foods that we find ourselves downing in larger quantities than we'd like, and for me, fig bars are in this column. Their not-quite-cookie-and-almost-real-food status speeds this along, and half a package of these chewy figgy lovelies can be gone before I've even realized what's happening. I think my fig bars are better than any that I can find in a bag—I really do. But miraculously, two is actually enough. Well, maybe three, but then I'm done.

FIG BARS MAKES FORTY-EIGHT 2-INCH COOKIES

FOR THE COOKIES

- ½ cup (1 stick) unsalted butter, at room temperature, plus extra for greasing the baking sheets

- 4 tablespoons (2 ounces) nonhydrogenated vegetable shortening (see page 217), at room temperature

- ½ cup (4 ounces) packed light brown sugar, homemade (page 51) or store-bought

- 2 large eggs

- 1 teaspoon Vanilla Extract, homemade (page 165) or store-bought

- 2 cups (10 ounces) all-purpose flour, plus extra for the counter

- ½ cup (2.25 ounces) whole wheat flour

- ½ teaspoon salt

- 1½ teaspoons baking powder

FOR THE FILLING

- 12 ounces dried Kalamata figs, hard stems snipped off

- 2 tablespoons fresh lemon juice (from 1 lemon)

- 2 tablespoons maple syrup

- ¼ teaspoon ground cinnamon

- ¼ teaspoon ground cardamom

1 **MAKE THE COOKIES.** Cream the butter, shortening, and brown sugar in the bowl of a mixer fit with the paddle attachment. When the mixture is light and fluffy, add the eggs one at a time, beating after each addition. Then add the vanilla and beat one more time.

2 In a separate mixing bowl, whisk together the flours, salt, and baking powder. Add the flour mixture to the egg mixture in two batches, mixing well after each addition. Use a spatula to scrape down the sides of the bowl, let the mixer do its work for another 10 seconds, then separate the dough into two portions. Wrap both balls of dough in plastic wrap or waxed paper and refrigerate for at least 2 hours, and up to overnight.

3 **MAKE THE FILLING.** Put the figs into a food processor and pulse to roughly chop. Add the lemon juice, maple syrup, cinnamon, cardamom, and 1 cup of water. Process for at least 30 seconds, until the filling is uniform. Transfer the mixture to a medium saucepan and set over medium heat. Add ¾ cup water and bring to a boil, stirring frequently. Cook at a low boil for 5 minutes, then remove from the heat and let cool.

4 Take the balls of dough out of the fridge and let them soften for 20 minutes. Preheat the oven to 375°F, and lightly grease two baking sheets.

5 Use a rolling pin to roll out the first ball of dough on a floured counter. It should be about ⅛ inch thick, and as close to a rectangle as you can muster. Use a knife to cut away any irregular edges, and then you should have a large rectangle. Gather the scraps you trimmed away, press them into a ball, wrap in plastic or waxed paper, and refrigerate.

6 Cut the rectangle into strips, each about 4 inches wide. Use a spoon to spread a line of filling about 1 inch wide down the center of each strip. Then, working with one strip at a time, fold the long sides of the strip over the filling and pinch them together where they meet in the middle. Repeat with the remaining dough strips. You should now have several long tubes of fig bar. Cut each tube into 2-inch cookies. Lay the cookies on one of the baking sheets seam side down, leaving about 2 inches of space between each one. Repeat with the second ball of dough, and then with the ball of trimmed edges you have in the refrigerator.

7 Bake the cookies for 18 to 20 minutes, or until they start to brown. Cool the cookies on a wire rack. They'll have a bit of crunch on the first day, but they'll soften up perfectly on the second day.

storage

ROOM TEMPERATURE • covered container, 1 week

FREEZER • freezer bag, 3 months (thaw at room temperature)

aFTER YEARS OF TALKING about buying a tent, Joey and I finally bought one. Within hours of our tent's arrival, we put it up in the backyard. Air mattresses inflated, sleeping bags zipped, and the LED lantern hung. The girls read books and played Candyland in the tent the whole afternoon. Then we slept in it.

I wouldn't call that first night a success. Our air mattress wasn't inflated enough, and by midnight my whole body ached. It was too hot, then too cold, and then at three o'clock in the morning, Sadie had to pee. When she asked if she could just go to sleep in her own bed, I gave up and went into mine as well. Joey and Rosie woke up well rested and plenty smug over their accomplishment.

Two weeks later we were on our way to Canada for a wedding, and it was time to give the tent a true go. I brought homemade marshmallows and graham crackers for our little fire. The marshmallows charred and smooshed, the chocolate melted just right, the graham crackers crunched, and we were all happy.

"I love camping." Rosie's mouth was stuffed, but I could still understand her.

The next morning, as we started to break down our tent, the sky opened up with the most torrential and driving rain I have ever experienced. I had to face the truth: I had carefully packed my misshapen homemade marshmallows and cinnamon graham crackers, but had neglected to bring a single raincoat.

Even though we showed up at the wedding in soggy clothes, we were quite proud of ourselves. Even so, I'll only go so far as to say that we're okay at camping. But s'mores? We're really good at that.

MARSHMALLOWS

- Canola oil for the pan and the knife

- *Optional:* 1 cup grated toasted unsweetened coconut or 1 cup powdered sugar

- 3 envelopes (¾ ounce) unflavored gelatin

- ½ cup granulated sugar

- ¾ cup Lyle's Golden Syrup (see page 63)

- ¼ teaspoon salt

- 1 teaspoon Vanilla Extract, homemade (page 165) or store-bought

variation ~
MARSHMALLOW FLUFF
Reduce the gelatin to 1 package. Transfer the mixture to the refrigerator after step 2.

1 Lightly grease a 9-inch square pan. If you are using toasted coconut, spread half of it into the bottom of the pan. Pour ⅔ cup water in the bowl of a stand mixer, then sprinkle the gelatin over the water. Let stand until the gelatin has turned from powder to gel, about 5 minutes.

2 Combine ½ cup water, the sugar, syrup, and salt in a medium saucepan. Clip a candy thermometer onto the side of the saucepan and cook over medium-high heat without stirring until the mixture reaches 250°F. Start the mixer on low speed with the wire whip attachment, and slowly and carefully add the hot syrup to the gelatin. Add the vanilla. Increase the speed on the mixer and beat for 10 to 15 minutes, or until the mixture becomes thick, bright white, and shiny.

3 Spread the mixture into your prepared pan and smooth out with a spatula. If using coconut, sprinkle the rest of it on top of the marshmallow layer. Let the marshmallows sit, uncovered at room temperature, for at least 12 hours. Turn the marshmallows out onto the counter, and with a greased knife, cut into 20 rectangles. If you want mini marshmallows, cut them into smaller pieces. If using powdered sugar, dust immediately before eating.

storage
ROOM TEMPERATURE • covered container, 3 weeks
FREEZER • freezer-safe container or bag, 3 months

---

tense moments ~ Yes, 10 to 15 minutes in the mixer seems like a lot. It will whir and whip forever, and you might think about losing hope that the mixture will ever become thick, bright white, and shiny, but don't lose hope! The transformation will be clear—the mixture will go from dull to glossy and thick, and it will happen.

a S A CHILD, "junk food" for me was carob-covered rice cakes and the occasional date-nut bar. I know I'm not alone, and the rest of you know who you are. I called the crispy end of the fried egg "bacon," and the candy that I snuck when my mother's back was turned was, in fact, cherry-flavored vitamin C. As I got older, I was sure that I would feed my children what I eventually learned the rest of the country was eating: real food from the supermarket.

My definition of "real food" has shifted a bit since then. Treats made of white sugar and chocolate are a common event around here, but the ingredients in store-bought junk food are often too scary for me to eat, let alone feed my kids. Joey was raised exclusively on pizza, Taco Bell, and Coca-Cola, but after eating the food that comes out of our kitchen for the last few years, even he gets ill on the other stuff. He will, however, always love his junk food, and so now we re-create those favorites at home, too.

In my search for a homemade sandwich cookie, most recipes have lacked one vital element. To truly replace those cookies that so many people claim as their only junk-food indulgence, the cookie must be black. It must be crunchy. It must get stuck in the teeth. The joy of the cookie is that no one can sneak one; the moment people open their mouths to deny the presence of the cookie, their black-lined teeth give them away.

The cookie that sandwiches the cream here is adapted from a cocoa wafer from *Pure Dessert* (Artisan, 2007) by the empress of chocolate, Alice Medrich. The cookie itself will also work in any recipe that calls for a store-bought chocolate wafer, like an icebox cake or a chocolate cookie crust.

THE SANDWICH COOKIE MAKES 40 TO 50 COOKIES

FOR THE COOKIES

- 1½ cups (7.5 ounces) all-purpose flour
- ¾ cup unsweetened cocoa powder
- ½ cup granulated sugar
- ½ teaspoon salt
- ¼ teaspoon baking soda
- 14 tablespoons (1¾ sticks) unsalted butter, at room temperature, cut into 1-inch chunks
- 3 tablespoons whole milk
- 1 teaspoon Vanilla Extract, homemade (page 165) or store-bought

FOR THE FILLING

- 4 tablespoons (½ stick) unsalted butter, at room temperature
- 4 tablespoons (2 ounces) nonhydrogenated vegetable shortening (see page 217)
- 1½ cups powdered sugar
- ¼ teaspoon salt
- 1 tablespoon Vanilla Extract, homemade (page 165) or store-bought

1 **MAKE THE COOKIES.** Combine the flour, cocoa powder, sugar, salt, and baking soda in a food processor and pulse several times until completely combined. Add the butter and pulse until the mixture is uniform. Combine the milk and vanilla in a small cup. With the food processor running, slowly add the milk mixture to the batter, continuing to process until the batter clumps around the blade.

2 Lay a large piece of waxed paper on the counter and put the batter onto it. Gently press the soft batter into a log about 2 inches in diameter. Wrap the batter in waxed paper, lay it into a paper towel roll that has been cut in half lengthwise, and roll the log in the paper towel roll. Put the log (in the paper towel roll) in the refrigerator for at least 1 hour.

3 Preheat the oven to 350°F. Line two baking sheets with parchment paper. Remove the log from the fridge, lay it on a cutting board, and take it out of the paper towel roll and waxed paper. Cut the log into slices that are as thin as you can make them, catching each slice as you go and laying it on the baking sheet, leaving 1 inch between cookies. Try for ⅛-inch slices, but it's okay if they are up to ¼ inch.

4 Bake the cookies for 12 to 15 minutes, rotating the baking sheets and switching their location halfway through baking. The cookies will puff up, then deflate, and they are done about 1 minute after they deflate. Transfer the cookies to a wire rack and continue to bake the remainder of the cookies, reusing the parchment paper. Cool entirely before filling. Unfilled cookies can now be stored.

5 **MAKE THE FILLING.** *If using the stand mixer,* combine the butter, shortening, powdered sugar, salt, and vanilla in the mixer bowl and beat together using the paddle until smooth and creamy. *If mixing by hand,* combine the ingredients in a mixing bowl and whisk until smooth and creamy.

6 Use a butter knife to spread about ½ inch of filling on one cookie. Top with a second cookie. Repeat.

storage

ROOM TEMPERATURE • filled cookies, covered container, 5 days; unfilled chocolate cookies, covered container, 2 weeks

FRIDGE • filling only, covered container, 10 days

FREEZER • freezer-safe container or bag, 3 months (just as good out of freezer as at room temperature; store whole batch in freezer, and take out individual cookies when you want them)

WHIPPED CREAM
—or—
sweetness

mY GRANDMOTHER is always with me in the kitchen. I don't have any convictions about what the afterlife might be, but I know that some part of her stands at the counter whenever I do.

I have never known someone who enjoyed food as my grandmother did. She and my grandfather ran a vegetarian, whole-grain bed and breakfast for the last fifteen years of her life, and while guests swooned over their garden frittatas and buckwheat pancakes, those weren't the dishes that really got her going. It was a transformative experience to sit at the table with my grandmother when she was involved in her rare indulgence in pork ribs. She would moan with joy with every bite, exclaiming over the perfection of the dish in front of her. She taught me about the bliss of an ideal snack in the middle of a day, sculpting waves of cream cheese on butter crackers before topping them with green olives. Although I know that as for most people, food can be a complicated and loaded subject, she embraced it with all her being, and she loved to feed others.

Food is always about much more than the food itself—so many aspects of how we live are expressed on our plates. My mother taught me how to make the best of what is in front of me. She can create a comforting meal from an empty fridge, and that resourcefulness runs through everything she does. In the end, the challenge of what to make for dinner with what is in the refrigerator and how to live well are connected: often the ingredients are right in front of us.

Life is too short to eat food that doesn't taste good. And if nothing else, let's eat *real* whipped cream. I think that my grandmother made whipped cream sometimes just so I could lick the beaters. Her joy was so palpable when she handed one to me. "Sweetness for my sweetness," she would say, and I would stand there next to her at the counter, licking every bit of that most wonderful cream from the beater.

WHIPPED CREAM   MAKES 2 CUPS

Place a metal mixing bowl or the bowl of a stand mixer in the freezer for 15 minutes. Remove the bowl from the freezer, and add the cream, maple syrup, and vanilla. Beat with the mixer or by hand with a whisk until the cream starts to thicken. Taste and adjust for sweetness. Continue beating until the cream holds soft peaks, 1 to 2 minutes.

- 1 cup heavy cream
- 1 tablespoon maple syrup, or more to taste
- 1 teaspoon Vanilla Extract, homemade (page 165) or store-bought

storage
FRIDGE · covered container, 4 hours
FREEZER · no

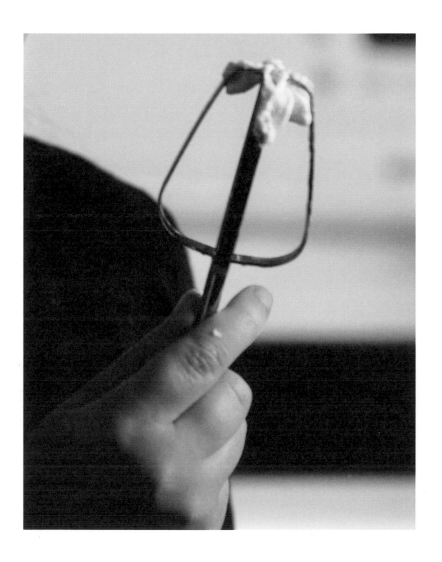

ACKNOWLEDGMENTS

Thank you.

To my agent, Rob Weisbach, for taking the leap into all of this with such love, skill, and grace. For being a superhero in every way.

To Jennifer May, for your photos that make me see the beauty in everything. For your steadiness, clear head, and for the love that you pour into your images.

To my editor Emily Takoudes, and to Doris Cooper, Peggy Paul, Lauren Shakely, and everyone else at Clarkson Potter, including Jane Treuhaft, Stephanie Huntwork, Carole Berglie, Ada Yonenaka, Kate Tyler, Anna Mintz, Sarah Breivogel, Allison Malec, Donna Passannante, and Hilary Sims. I showed up at the Random House building terrified, and I was immediately surrounded by wonderful women who all wanted to talk about recipes. You are my kind of people.

To Audrey Sussman, for testing every one of these recipes in your kitchen with all of your savvy, experience, and sense of humor.

To Chandler Crawford and Jo Grossman. This book would have never made it out of my kitchen without you.

To Kari Chapin, for your extraordinary sense of style, and for finding objects filled with meaning for every page of this book. For telling me that anything I wanted was possible, and for helping me make it happen.

To Jessica Bard, for your expertise, creativity, and for sharing your kitchen with us.

To Eilen Jewell, for showing me how to do what I love for a living. To Sarah Yanni, for feeding both my heart and my belly. To Molly de St. Andre, for your love and art. To Lissa McGovern, for every single thing. To Hedley Stone and Zoe Mizuho, for bringing so much magic into our house during the year that this book came to be. To Aurel de St. Andre, for your breathtaking designs and your fabulous crepes. To Janet Elsbach, for constant inspiration, and for the secret canning army in your kitchen. To Paige Orloff, my favorite writer. And to all our friends who fill our lives, our table, and these pages with so much love. To Meg Eisenhauer Barry, Alice Goldfarb, Jefferson Navicky, Brandee and Chris Nelson, Jason Beek, Nancy Wilkinson, Megan Sielken and Ben Ransford, Dave and Amarah Bailey, Cea and Jon Catuccio, Marya La Roche, Naomi and Ron Blumenthal, Luke Meyer and India Adams, Bruce and Amy Humes, Erin and Ian Maxwell, Thom Barry, and Luke Kirkland and Caroline Golden.

To Andrew Smith, for knowing exactly what I wanted to say.

To Chris Metze, Eric Nixon, Callum Benepe, David DeRosa, Greg Takoudes, and Mitchell Smilowitz for supporting their partners through the making of this book.

To Bridie Clark, for her warmth, wit, and generosity.

To all the farmers who provided food for the recipes and photos in this book. Thanks to my friends Al Thorpe and Elizabeth Keen of Indian Line Farm, and to Jen and Pete Salinetti of Woven Roots Farm, Paul Paisley and the Jersey cows of Twin Oaks Farm, and Sean Stanton of North Plain and Blue Hill Farms; to Gould Farm in Monterey, Massachusetts; Thompson Finch Farm in Ancramdale, New York; Love Apple Farm in Ghent, New York; and Windy Hill Orchards in Great Barrington, Massachusetts.

And to all of the artists who shared their work for the photographs in this book—to Moho designs for their stunning silkscreened textiles; to Naomi Blumenthal, R Wood Studios; Molly de St. Andre, Daniel Bellow, and Karissa Chase for their pottery; to Alan Young at The Sow's Ear for his perfect wooden spreader; and to Cardinale Montano for her artful woolens. To Germain for their vintage fabrics, to Mark Firth for his lovely tortilla press, to Amy for her favorite plate from Paris, and to Kelly for her warm fire.

To the fabulous supporting cast of recipe testers: Megan Sielken, Cindy Rosenbaum, Teresa Lee, and Kelly Bancroft. To C. J. Walton, Michele DiSimone, and Audrey Sussman for sharing their recipes. To the Denver Chernilas. To Ricki Carroll and Sandor Katz. To my neighbor Hannah, for always lending me butter.

To Shirley and Irving Yost, for their whole-grain pancakes and for being ahead of the trend, and to Courtney Hunt, for convincing me to do impossible things. To Laurie Colwin, Mollie Katzen, Alice Waters, and to the readers of Eatingfromthegroundup.com, who keep me going.

To my mother and friend, Jamie, for teaching me to steam, fry, chop, and sing. For reading every word I have ever written. To my sister, Maia, for all that she is and will be. To my stepfather, Chris, who brings us all together with his kind heart.

And most of all, to Joey. For everything, and especially for saying yes that first time, and over again ever since. And to my girls, Sadie and Rosie. I am honored to be the one who gets to feed you. Thank you both just for being who you are.

INDEX